REPENTANCE

AND
GRACE

Rediscovering the Bible's
Simple, Harmonious Teaching

REPENTANCE
AND
GRACE

Rediscovering the Bible's
Simple, Harmonious Teaching

Douglas Daudelin

W

Word Of Grace And Truth
P.O. Box 325, Allamuchy, NJ 07820-0325

To the one who earnestly seeks
the God of the Bible,
that you may not be led astray by persuasive words—
but that you may grow in the knowledge and love of God, and
that you may be filled with the fruits of righteousness through Jesus Christ,
that He may be satisfied with the labor of His soul,
to the glory and praise of God.

Contents

Chapter 1

Introduction

*The Lord is ... not willing that any should perish
but that all should come to repentance.*
—2 Peter 3:9

For by grace you have been saved through faith.
—Ephesians 2:8

The two verses quoted above show how important repentance and grace are to Christianity. Repentance and grace are two pillars of the Christian faith. And yet, we find these pillars in terrible disrepair in today's preaching.

Repentance is largely ignored. In many churches, it is uncommon to hear the word mentioned, even though Jesus told us that repentance should be preached in His name to all nations (Luke 24:47). And whenever the word *is* mentioned, it is usually left unexplained; and should it be explained, it is often misrepresented. Misunderstandings about repentance extend also to its relationship with other important doctrines—not only grace, but also faith, the gospel, salvation, sanctification, and others. As a result, there is considerable confusion about repentance, and it is often not even brought to mind.

Conversely, grace is preached frequently, and Christians know it is of utmost importance. But the Bible warns us that *"certain persons have crept in unnoticed ... who turn the grace of our God into licentiousness [a disregard of moral restraints]"* (Jude 4 NASB). And many misunderstand grace in ways that make it appear there is tension between grace and what is variously represented as repentance. They may be puzzled when they consider how the two verses quoted at the top of this chapter can be reconciled, or they are unsure of interpretations they have heard which contrive to do so.

The pillars of grace and repentance provide a significant foundation for many other doctrines. We can think of other doctrines as being built together into a structure that rests in part on these pillars. However, because their deteriorated condition prevents them from providing the proper support, problems are appearing throughout the structure: some parts do not align properly, others have cracks in them, etc.

This state of affairs is having a grave impact on Christians individually, affecting their personal walks as well as their understanding and sharing of the gospel. Misunderstandings about repentance and grace are also at the root of numerous controversies among churches—fracturing the evangelical community. Must we repent to be saved? And what, exactly, is repentance? Differing notions of what repentance means, and whether it is necessary, underlie many of those contentions. Yet the disputes may not be framed as being rooted in differing views of repentance. And the different ideas about repentance are often influenced by doctrines of grace.

Jesus described our need to get the foundation right when building (Luke 6:48-49). In the light of Jesus' instruction, *Repentance and Grace* seeks to repair this foundation. Its remedy is to rediscover the Bible's simple and harmonious teaching about repentance and grace.

We will address the heart of these issues by developing a good understanding of repentance from the Bible alone. Then, we will ask the question, "What about grace?" Carefully looking again to the Scriptures for the answer reveals the harmony between repentance and grace that we know must exist in those inspired words. That harmony came at an awful cost to God—the sacrifice of His Son for our sins.

This book does not attempt to represent or defend the doctrines of any theological system or denomination, and it is free of denominational jargon and presuppositions. Its purpose is to show and explain the Bible's teaching about these two pillars of our faith, clearly and unambiguously, and to do so using the language of the Scriptures. Although the analysis here is careful and extensive, the Bible's teaching about repentance and grace is wonderfully simple. Quotations from the Scriptures are printed in italics (and in book formats printed in color, they are also shown in red) so that readers may more easily distinguish and refer to those words of truth when evaluating what is said about them.

To accomplish its purpose, this book takes a straightforward path. It begins with a short chapter giving background information that is helpful for anyone to have who would like to come to a better understanding of something in the Bible. The background chapter also includes introductory information about the importance of repentance and what it means in the New Testament. The chapter that follows it describes some basic relationships between repentance and faith, the gospel, and salvation.

The next four chapters thoroughly describe biblical repentance—showing from the Bible what it is, and what it is not, and whether we may later turn from repentance. Common misunderstandings and objections are addressed along the way and also in immediately subsequent chapters.

After developing a faithful and detailed understanding of the Bible's teaching on repentance, we will explore grace in the New Testament. The first of these chapters simply and easily explains the harmonious relationship between grace and repentance. The remaining chapters then expound upon God's amazing grace as now revealed to us in the New Testament—with its blessings and promises, and our fitting and required response. In those chapters, the meaning of *grace* in the New Testament is defined and extensively demonstrated.

Chapter 2

Background

Who is the LORD, *that I should obey His voice?*
— Exodus 5:2

Any time we seek to understand something God has communicated to us in the Bible, it is helpful to know certain basic truths about both God and the Scriptures. Those truths include who God is, the nature of the Scriptures, and the faithfulness of translations to the words originally penned by the prophets and apostles. That background is provided here in a nutshell. On the way, we will begin to see how important repentance is to the New Covenant. The last section briefly describes repentance.

2.1 Who Is God?
Our universe is immense and contains a tremendous amount of matter. More than one million earths could fit inside our sun, which is considered a medium-sized star among the estimated 100 to 400 billion stars found in just our galaxy, the Milky Way.[1] And astronomers today estimate there are hundreds of billions of galaxies in the universe.[2]

---

[1] How Many Stars in the Milky Way? (2015). *NASA Blueshift*. Retrieved August 13, 2022, from https://asd.gsfc.nasa.gov/blueshift/index.php/2015/07/22/how-many-stars-in-the-milky-way/

[2] Hubble Reveals Observable Universe Contains 10 Times More Galaxies Than Previously Thought (2017). *NASA*. Retrieved August 13, 2022, from https://www.nasa.gov/feature/goddard/2016/hubble-reveals-observable-universe-contains-10-times-more-galaxies-than-previously-thought

It should be apparent that the things we see all around us on the earth and in the universe have not existed forever. For instance, we know the sun and stars have not been burning *forever* (since even nuclear "fires" consume their fuel). Then, where did all of this come from? And if someone has an answer,[3] then where did *that* come from?

At the end of the answers to such a line of questioning (this came from that, and that came from this other, which itself came from something else…), we must eventually arrive at something which we believe did not come into being through anything else—something which existed from all eternity past, and from which everything else has come into existence (whatever that might be).

The Bible's answer to that question is found in its first verse: "*In the beginning God created the heavens and the earth*" (Gen. 1:1). Our universe began when God created it. And before He created it, He existed. He **was** "*in the beginning.*" Nothing and no one created Him. As Psalm 90:2 describes, "*Before the mountains were brought forth, or ever You had formed the earth and the world, even **from** everlasting **to** everlasting, You are God.*"

Perhaps that is a reason one of God's unique names is "*I AM.*"[4] And God created everything else that exists in "*the heavens and the earth.*" John 1:3 explains, "*All things came into being through Him, and without Him not even one thing came into being that has come into being*" (LITV).

In Exodus 5:2, Pharaoh asked Moses, "***Who is the Lord, that I should obey His voice?***" The words Moses wrote in the first verse of the Bible answer that important question. They tell us the most significant thing a person can know about God and all that we see.

That was also the first thing Paul told the Athenians about the God of the Bible in his preaching recorded in Acts 17:22–31. After mentioning that he had seen among their objects of worship an altar "*TO AN UNKNOWN GOD,*" he began to tell them about God by

---

[3] For example, "An initial singularity."
[4] See Ex. 3:13–14 and John 8:58 in the NKJV.

16

saying, *"Not knowing, then, whom you worship, I make Him known to you. The God who made the world and all things in it, this One being Lord of Heaven and of earth..."* (vv. 23–24 LITV). Because God created all things, He is Lord over them all.

Moses reminded Israel of who God is when he began to set God's law before them in Deuteronomy 4. Then, he described why that knowledge should make them careful to obey His voice: *"**Know** therefore today, and **take it to your heart**, that the LORD, He is God in heaven above and on the earth below; there is no other. **So** you shall keep His statutes and His commandments which I am giving you today, that it may go well with you and with your children after you"* (vv. 39–40 NASB). Pharaoh did not obey God's voice, and it surely did not go well with him or his children.

2.2 The Nature of the Scriptures

If someone who knows nothing about God were to read just one verse out of the entire Old Testament, a good choice might well be Genesis 1:1. It is no accident that such a significant statement about God is in the Bible's first verse; for God both *chose*, and *ordered*, *all the words* in the Scriptures.

We might find evidence of this in "Strong's numbers." Those numbers are defined in Strong's famous dictionaries of the words in the Old and New Testament texts in the original languages.[5] In each dictionary, Strong assigned a number to each of the words, sequentially numbering them in alphabetical order. Consider the following highly improbable "coincidence." Out of all the Hebrew (and some Aramaic) words in the Old Testament, the one which is first in alphabetical order—the one which is given Strong's #1—is the Hebrew word for **Father** (Isa. 63:16; 64:8). And out of all the Greek words in the New Testament, the one with Strong's #1 is the Greek letter "**A**"—a letter which is used as a word to refer to **Jesus**

---

[5] James Strong, *Dictionary of the Hebrew Bible*, and *Dictionary of the Greek Testament* (New York, NY: The Methodist Book Concern, 1890). Both dictionaries are reprinted (among many other places) in *Strong's Exhaustive Concordance* (Grand Rapids, MI: Baker Book House, 1989, ISBN 0-8010-8108-4).

(Rev. 1:8; 21:6; 22:13).[6]

The Bible is not the mere words of numerous human authors who wrote according to their imperfect understandings over more than a thousand years. It is the words of God revealing what is true: *"Know this **first of all**, that **no** prophecy of Scripture ... was **ever** made by an act of human will, but men moved by the Holy Spirit spoke from God"* (2 Pet. 1:20–21 NASB)—*"All Scripture is inspired by God"* (2 Tim. 3:16 NASB).

Accordingly, Paul wrote to the Christians in Thessalonica, *"For our exhortation did not come from **error** or **uncleanness**, nor was it in **deceit**. ... For this reason we also thank God without ceasing, because when you received the word of God which you heard from us, you welcomed it **not as the word of men**, but as it is in truth, **the word of God"** (1 Thess. 2:3, 13).

It is not the purpose of this book to provide evidence that the Bible is *"in truth, the word of God."* Rather, this book examines and describes what the Bible teaches about repentance and grace with the understanding that it is the word of God. Nevertheless, in doing so, we will naturally encounter passages in the Bible which state, or provide evidence of, or demonstrate its nature.

Indeed, if we believe in the Jesus who is described in the Scriptures, we should also believe all that those Scriptures tell us. For Jesus called the writers of the Scriptures *"prophets"* (Matt. 26:56; see also Luke 18:31), and rebuked some of His disciples in Luke 24:25 by saying, *"O foolish ones, and slow of heart to believe in **all** that the prophets have spoken!"* When Jesus said that, He implicitly made clear they also **had** what the prophets have spoken.

In John 8:47, Jesus said, *"The one who is of God hears the Words of God,"* and those who *"do not hear ... are not of God"* (LITV).

---

[6] The letter is found in the Textus Receptus text, but is replaced by the name of the letter (transliterated in English *alpha*) in some Greek texts.

2.3 The First Word of New Testament Preaching

With that understanding of the nature of the words in the Bible, it is interesting to ask, "What is the first word of preaching recorded in the New Testament?" It should not surprise us to discover that word has special significance to the New Testament.

The first word of preaching is found in the beginning of Matthew chapter 3, and it is "*Repent.*" We read in verses 1–2, "*In those days John the Baptist came preaching in the wilderness of Judea, and saying, 'Repent...'.*" That aspect of John's message is not unexpected, since Mark 1:4 tells us that he was "*preaching a baptism of repentance for the forgiveness of sins*" (NASB). God ushered in the New Covenant with the preaching of repentance.

We will see that repentance does indeed have special significance to the New Testament. Hebrews 6:1–2 is one passage which shows that significance. It lists things that are said to be a foundation and "*the first principles of the oracles of God*" (Heb. 5:12). Not only is repentance one of them, but it is listed first. It comes ahead of faith, the resurrection of the dead, and eternal judgment!

2.4 The First Word of Jesus' Preaching

But someone will ask, "What is the first word of *Jesus'* preaching recorded in the New Testament?" That is found in Matthew 4:17: "*Jesus began to preach and to say, 'Repent...'.*" The New Testament was written in Greek, and the Greek word used there for "*Repent*" is the same Greek word and inflection[7] as the first word of John's recorded preaching: μετανοεῖτε. It is inflected as a second person plural, present active imperative. We could render the sense of that inflection in English explicitly as, "I command you all now to repent."

---

[7] An inflection is a specific form of a word, often involving at least the construction of its ending, used to express grammatical attributes such as tense, person, and number. Greek words typically have multiple inflections. Note that Strong's dictionaries show and number only the lexical form of a word, not the various inflected forms of that word. An English analogue would be a number for the word "run" that is used to denote not only "run," but also "runs," "ran," and "running."

Consistent with that rendering of Jesus' command, the final words Paul preached to the Athenians in the passage from Acts 17 were, *"God ... now commands all men everywhere to repent, because He has appointed a day on which He will judge the world in righteousness by the Man whom He has ordained. He has given assurance of this to all by raising Him from the dead"* (vv. 30–31).

2.5 Faithful Translations

If you want to know and understand what God has communicated to us in the Bible and you read an English translation of the Bible, you should satisfy yourself that it is a **faithful representation** of the Greek and Hebrew words that God wrote to us through the prophets and apostles. There are two issues here: whether the words God wrote for our instruction have been preserved, and whether a particular English translation faithfully represents those words.

There are more than five thousand ancient Greek manuscripts that are copies or portions of the New Testament.[8] Together, they consist of more than two million pages.[9, 10] Those manuscripts are from different geographical regions and time periods. Comparing them confirms that the original Greek text has been reliably preserved, since differences between them are minor or inconsequential.[11]

---

[8] Josh McDowell, *Evidence That Demands a Verdict—Volume 1: Historical Evidences for the Christian Faith* (San Bernardino, CA: Here's Life Publishers, 1989), 39.

[9] JMM Team, Testing the Historical Reliability of the New Testament (2018). *Josh McDowell Ministry*. Retrieved August 13, 2022, from https://www.josh.org/historical-reliability-new-testament/

[10] The Institute for New Testament Textual Research at the University of Münster in Germany provides an online, *New Testament Virtual Manuscript Room* (retrieved August 13, 2022 from https://ntvmr.uni-muenster.de/home) where New Testament manuscripts can be listed and viewed.

[11] McDowell wrote in *Evidence That Demands a Verdict*, p. 44, *"Philip Schaff in Comparison to the Greek Testament and the English Version* concluded that only 400 ... variant readings caused doubt about the textual meaning, and only 50 of these were of great significance. Not one of the variations, Schaff says, altered 'an article of faith or a precept of duty which is not abundantly sustained by other and undoubted passages, or by the

However, do not mistakenly think this kind of confirmation is necessary. Although it is not a subject of this book, here are three brief reasons we can know God has preserved the words He wrote for us:

1. God said He would (Ps. 12:6–7; Isa. 59:21; Prov. 22:19–21).
2. At the time Jesus came into the world, He made clear that the Old Testament had been reliably preserved (John 10:34–35; Luke 24:25–27; 16:29; John 5:39, 46–47; He also fulfilled many prophecies in it).
3. The Scriptures themselves should show a person who carefully studies them that they are evidently the uncorrupted words of God revealing truth, not the corrupted words of many imperfect men (Prov. 8:6–9; John 7:46, 16–18; 8:28; Eph. 3:3–4).

Nevertheless, when it comes to producing an English translation of those words, translators may have an imperfect, incomplete, or incorrect understanding of a passage's meaning.[12] Therefore, your English version should not have been produced with the purpose of expressing what its translators have interpreted (or worse, would *like*) the **meaning** of each verse or passage to be. Such **interpretations** and opinions belong in commentaries or footnotes. When translators attempt to convey their opinion of a passage's **meaning**, the true teaching may easily be lost.

Your English version should be a faithful **translation**—a version that has endeavored to translate the Greek **words** that were written in the New Testament as closely as possible into English. Put simply, you should want an English version in which you can read the words of God, not the fallible opinions (or preferences) of others about the

---

whole tenor of Scripture teaching.'" About his personal experience, McDowell wrote on p. 73, "After trying to shatter the historicity and validity of the Scripture, I came to the conclusion that it is historically trustworthy."

[12] After all, even those who wrote the Scriptures did not always understand what they were writing. Some passages which show that are 1 Pet. 1:10–12, Dan. 12:8–9, and 1 Cor. 8:2. Nevertheless, they faithfully penned what God directed them to write.

words of God.

Jesus taught us the importance of knowing every word that has come from God's mouth when He said that man will not live by bread alone *"but by every word that proceeds from the mouth of God"* (Matt. 4:4). If someone does not choose to study a faithful translation of those words, that person has effectively chosen to trust what some particular group of people says about God's word. Further, that person has disregarded Jesus' teaching about what is necessary for a man to live.

Isaiah 8:20 tells us how we should evaluate the statements and interpretations of others: *"To the law and to the testimony! If they do not speak according to this word, it is because there is no light in them."* The expression *"the law and ... the testimony"* in this verse refers to the Scriptures. When someone brings a teaching that is new to us, we should try to discern whether it is compatible with the Scriptures.[13] For if it is incompatible, then the teaching is not true.

Only if you have a faithful translation, and are familiar with it, are you equipped to apply this test from Isaiah 8. Otherwise, you are prey to being led by the blind (Matt. 15:14). Jesus told the Sadducees a reason they had major errors in their beliefs was because they were not familiar with the Scriptures, saying, *"You are mistaken, not knowing the Scriptures"* (Matt. 22:29).

2.6 A Brief Description of Repentance

In later chapters, we will look carefully at the Bible's teaching about repentance, particularly in the New Testament. This section gives a brief but precise description of repentance without proving or expounding upon it here. Having this background understanding should make it easier to follow and evaluate the passages and reasoning presented in subsequent chapters while they develop a fuller understanding of repentance.

In the Old Testament, *repent* is used to refer to "changing your purposes." God's statement in Jeremiah 4:28 neatly illustrates this

---

[13] For a good example of this, see Acts 17:11.

meaning: "*I have* **purposed** *and I will* **not repent** *[I will not change My purpose], nor will I* **turn** *back from it*" (LITV).

In the New Testament, *repent* also refers to changing your purposes, but it is **exclusively** used in the way we customarily think of it: changing from purposes that are morally bad to those that are morally good (in one or more matters). In other words, to repent is to change your purposes from purposing to sin to purposing to do what God wants you to do. Here is a good summary of the meaning of the verb *repent* as it is used in the New Testament: to change your purposes to a resolve to do God's will.

The meaning of the noun *repentance* in the New Testament is, "Changed purposes to a resolve to obey God."[14] Equivalently, it is a resolve to follow Jesus.[15] True repentance has a plain and true resolve. It is not qualified with caveats such as "I'll obey God *unless* (or *if*) this, that, or the other thing are the case."

The New Testament tells us that grief over our sins may **lead to** repentance. Therefore, those remorseful feelings are distinguished

---

[14] *The Westminster Confession of Faith*, written in the mid-1600's, in chapter XV ("Of Repentance Unto Life") section II, says of repentance, "By it, a sinner ... **turn**[s] from them **all** [his sins] unto God, **purposing** and endeavoring to walk with Him in **all** the ways of His commandments." [Emphasis added. The ellipsis replaces text describing *motivation* for the quoted turning, purposing, and endeavoring (and its description of that motivation appears to portray it as necessary to true repentance). Note that this and all other quotations in this book which are not from the Scriptures are not intended to be taken as proving what the Bible teaches nor the truth of any statement or doctrine. As it is written, "*Rather, let God be found true, though every man be found a liar*" (Rom. 3:4 NASB). Indeed, *The Westminster Confession of Faith* itself, in chapter XXXI section III, says, "All synods or councils, since the Apostles' times, whether general or particular, may err; and many have erred. Therefore they are not to be made the rule of faith, or practice."] Reprinted in *Trinity Hymnal* (Suwanee, GA: Great Commission Publications, Twenty-first printing, 2008), 680, 688.

[15] A resolve to follow Jesus is equivalent in effect to a resolve to do God's will, and they can be used interchangeably. For in John 5:30 Jesus said, "*I do not seek My own will but the will of the Father who sent Me.*" And in John 8:29 Jesus told us, "*I always do those things that please Him.*"

from repentance, and are not included in the given definition of *repentance*. Although we will see that true faith and repentance always come together (not to say at the same instant), repentance is also different from faith.

We are told that a result or **fruit** of repentance is works. Therefore, repentance, like faith, is not a work. So works are also excluded from the definition of *repentance*.

As the New Testament uses the word *repentance*, it is simply and only a **resolve**—a matter of the heart and will. It is a resolve to obey God.

Acknowledging your sins is not repenting; though inwardly acknowledging some of one's sins must precede repentance.[16] Outwardly confessing a sin is also not included in the definition of *repentance*, though it may be a fruit of repentance.

Repenting is often described or referred to in both Old and New Testaments as *turning*. That is demonstrated in the quoted verse from Jeremiah 4:28. Like changed purposes, *turning* has to do with changing the *intended direction* or path of your steps going forward, but is not the steps themselves. It concerns the goal and desired destination of your walking. It is the heart and will that **turn**. Of course, if you have truly changed the direction in which you intend to walk, the fruits of that repentance will be steps taken in the new direction.

In general, a person turns **from** one thing **to** another. For example, a person may "*turn* **from** *darkness* **to** *light*" and "*repent and turn* **to** *God*" (Acts 26:18, 20 NASB). In the same way, repenting consists of changing your purposes **from** one set **to** another.

As used in the New Testament, the resolve of repentance is to obey God in any matter and, therefore, in every matter. As a result, unlike

---

[16] Otherwise, what is one repenting from?

faith,[17] there is no spectrum or degree of repentance. In the New Testament, a person either has or does not have repentance—one is either repentant or unrepentant. This true "New Testament" repentance is also described as *"repentance unto life"* (Acts 11:18 LITV) and *"repentance to salvation"* (2 Cor. 7:10 LITV).

People may repent from specific sins, resolving to turn from them to do God's will in those specific areas. In a small number of New Testament verses that use *repent*, what should be repented from or to is explicitly mentioned.[18]

However, in all other New Testament verses where *repent* is found, including every verse in which there is a command to repent,[19] it means to resolve to do God's will in every matter. Therefore, the command to repent in the New Testament is a command to put oneself in, or restore oneself to, the state of being repentant.

This usage in the New Testament is one common meaning today of the English word *repent*, as reflected in the first definition given in *Merriam-Webster's Dictionary and Thesaurus*: "To **turn from sin** and **resolve** to reform one's **life** [emphasis added]."[20]

---

[17] Two passages which show faith has degrees are Luke 17:5 and Rom. 12:3.
[18] For example, Rev. 2:21 and 16:9.
[19] For example, Acts 2:38 and 17:30.
[20] *Merriam-Webster's Dictionary and Thesaurus* (Springfield, MA: Merriam-Webster, 2007, ISBN 978-0-87779-640-4), 684.

Chapter 3

Repentance and the Gospel

Repentance and remission of sins should be preached
in His name to all nations.
—Luke 24:47

Salvation is a free gift that God gives by His grace (Rom. 3:23–24; 6:23; 5:15). There is nothing any sinful person can do to earn, achieve, or merit it. However, when people give gifts to one another, they do not give to everyone but have criteria by which they choose the recipients. The same is true of God.

To illustrate, James 4:6 describes grace which God gives to the humble but not the proud, "*God sets Himself against proud ones, but He gives grace to humble ones*" (LITV). In the same way, God does not give the gift of salvation indiscriminately.

We must believe in Jesus in order for God to save us. When the Philippian jailer asked Paul and Silas in Acts 16:30, "*What must I do to be saved?*" they answered, "*Believe in the Lord Jesus, and you will be saved*" (v. 31 NASB). Conversely, Jesus taught that those who do not believe in Him will perish in their sins: "*If you do not believe that I AM [one of God's unique names, as mentioned in section 2.1], you will die in your sins*" (John 8:24 LITV).

Likewise, we will see that we must repent in order for God to save us. After Peter had preached the gospel to a crowd in Acts chapter 2, when they asked Peter and the apostles, "*Brothers, what shall we do?*" (v. 37 LITV) Peter answered, "*Repent ... and you will receive the gift of the Holy Spirit*" (v. 38 NASB).[21] Conversely, Jesus taught that those who do not repent will perish in their sins: "*Unless you repent you will all likewise perish*" (Luke 13:5).[22]

Although believing and repenting are things the Bible tells us we must do in order for God to save us, paradoxically, the Bible also teaches that God gives both faith and repentance (Phil. 1:29; Matt. 16:15–17; Acts 14:27; 11:18; 5:31; 2 Tim. 2:25).[23] That man did well who cried out to Jesus with tears saying, "*Lord, I believe; help my unbelief!*" (Mark 9:24)

This chapter describes some basic relationships between repentance and faith, the gospel, and salvation.

3.1 Faith and Repentance—Perfected Together
Faith is different from repentance, but neither true faith nor repentance is found without the other. They come as a pair (not to say simultaneously). Although they are not synonymous, someone who has truly repented has faith. And someone who truly believes will repent.

Would anyone **resolve** to follow Jesus who does not **believe** in Him? Someone must have faith in Jesus in order to repent. It is not that if somehow people could be persuaded to resolve to follow Jesus regardless of the earthly consequences, afterward they will believe in Him. Rather, it is those who come to believe in Jesus who then repent and resolve to follow Him. Therefore, someone who has truly repented has faith.

---

[21] The content represented by the ellipsis, which does not change what is said in this verse about repenting to receive the gift of the Holy Spirit, is addressed at the end of this chapter.
[22] *The Westminster Confession of Faith*, in chapter XV section III, says, "Although repentance be not … any satisfaction for sin … none may expect pardon without it." *Trinity Hymnal*, 680.
[23] We will see a number of things which God, in His wisdom, has made paradoxical—combining two things that we would not have expected to see together or that we might have thought of as mutually exclusive.

In the chapter introduction, we read the statement, *"Believe in the Lord Jesus, and you will be saved"* (Acts 16:31 NASB). Then, where does repentance come in, and how is the answer compatible with this statement?

The short answer is that it comes in because someone who truly believes will also repent to be saved[24]—as they must to avoid perishing.[25] Accordingly, Peter answered those who had believed the gospel he had just preached, and asked what they should now do, by saying, *"Repent ... and you will receive the gift of the Holy Spirit"* (Acts 2:38 NASB).

We are told that God will save whoever **believes in Jesus** (John 3:16; Acts 16:31). But what does it mean to "believe in Jesus," and how is that faith linked to repentance? After outlining the answers to those two questions here, the answers will be expounded on in the rest of this chapter, quoting and discussing many of the verses referenced in this section.

Believe in the Lord Jesus

Note that the object of this faith is not a promise or a doctrine. It is the resurrected Lord Jesus Himself. The Scriptures tell us we must believe in **Him**. Believing *in Him* is not simply believing in Him "**for**" something, nor "**as**" something (though of course it includes some of those things).

The statement in Acts 16:31, *"Believe in the Lord Jesus,"* is far-reaching, and it does not describe some very important details. It must mean more than simply believing there is someone *named* Jesus about whom one knows nothing, or mistakenly holds some significantly wrong notions. Clearly, we must *hear* of Jesus in order to believe in Him. And those who truly believe in Him—who is *"the Savior of the world"* (John 4:42), *"nor is there salvation in any*

---

[24] As 2 Cor. 7:10 speaks of *"repentance to salvation"* (LITV).

[25] One of many passages that show repentance is necessary to have our sins forgiven and avoid perishing in them is Luke 13:5, quoted in this chapter's introduction.

other" (Acts 4:12)—will also call on Him to save them.

Jesus asked a (formerly) blind man whose eyes He had opened, "*Do you believe in the Son of God?*" and he well answered, "*Who is He, Lord, that I may believe in Him?*" (John 9:35–36)

When I was an unbeliever in my twenties, I visited a church on a special occasion. In his message, the pastor told about a young man who went to his pastor and told him that he had decided he did not believe in God. After talking with the young man for a short while about his decision, the pastor said he agreed with him—he did not believe in that God either. I left with a strong impression that God had tried to communicate to me that I did not know Him.

There are some people who say they believe in Jesus, but if asked to describe the Jesus in whom they believe, they describe someone different from the biblical Jesus. But the Jesus who is described in the Bible is the *only One* who died for them and can save them from their sins.

Believing in and calling on an imaginary Jesus to save you is futile. This is shown by a passage which begins in Romans 10:13 with the wonderful promise, "*Whoever calls on the name of the LORD shall be saved.*" But the next verse rhetorically asks, "*How then shall they call on Him in whom they have not believed? And how shall they believe in Him of whom they have not heard?*" The answer, of course, is that they cannot.

We need to be both careful and diligent then to make sure we know the Lord and Savior Jesus Christ in whom we must believe. As Jesus said in John 17:3, "*And this is eternal life, that they may know You, the only true God, and Jesus Christ whom You have sent.*"

Certainly, one must believe in the Jesus who is described in the Bible. But no one knows *everything* about Him. Then, what truths regarding "who He is" need to be known and believed in order to "*believe in Him*" (John 9:36) and be saved? The Scriptures show us that believing in Him includes believing at least these truths about Him: He is the Son of God (John 20:31), who is God (John 8:24;

Luke 18:18–19; John 1:1; 20:28–29) and the Christ (1 John 5:1), whom God raised from the dead (Rom. 10:9—He is a living Savior) after He died for our sins (1 Cor. 15:1, 3).

But the demons also know and believe these things about Him (James 2:19; Luke 4:34, 41; Mark 1:34; Acts 19:15). And they also know the time is coming when He will judge them for their rebellion against Him (Matt. 8:29; Luke 4:34)! James 2:19 assumes readers will naturally understand that true belief must consist of more than the demons' belief.

Just as *not all* disciples are "*truly*" Jesus' disciples, not all belief is acceptable to God (John 8:30–31 LITV). Not all who call Jesus "*Lord, Lord*" have *truly* believed in Him (Matt. 7:22–23)!

Believe Jesus' Words

Believing in Jesus also includes believing **what He has said** (John 12:48; 10:26–27). Expressed a different way, we could consider all of Jesus' teaching to be prefaced with, "If you believe in Me, believe this that I say to you: ...." Here again, no one knows or understands perfectly *all* that He has said (1 Cor. 8:2). But, especially because of who Jesus is, that faith includes a mindset that you *will* believe whatever you *may come* to understand He has said (John 6:67–69).

Importantly, this One in whom we must believe is different from anyone else in that He both knows all things (Job 37:16; 1 John 3:20) and cannot lie (Titus 1:2; Num. 23:19). Further, He has all authority in heaven and earth and is faithful to His word (Matt. 28:18; Ps. 119:89–91). Therefore, what He has spoken, He will make good (Num. 23:19).

Believe All the Words of God

Because of what Jesus said in John 8:47, believing in Jesus includes believing all of the *other* words written in the Bible for our instruction. As Jesus said, "*My brothers are these: the ones hearing the Word of God*" (Luke 8:21 LITV).[26] The psalmist expressed that all those words are true, as well as his personal belief of them, when he said, "*The entirety of Your word is truth*" (Ps. 119:160).

Believe That God Rewards Those Who Seek Him

Hebrews 11 has a lengthy description of faith and what it has caused those who believe in God to do. Verse 6 teaches that acceptable faith *must* include believing that God rewards those who diligently seek Him: "*He who comes to God **must believe** that He is, and that He is a rewarder of those who diligently seek Him.*"

One example of what faith and a belief that God rewards those who seek Him have caused people to do is given in verses 24–26: It was "***by faith***" that Moses chose to "*endure ill-treatment with the people of God*" and to deny himself "*the passing pleasures of sin*" **because** "*he was looking to the reward*" (NASB).

In terms of sheer physical effort and size, perhaps the greatest work ever done by someone because of faith is described in verse 7: "***By faith** Noah, being **warned** by God about things **not yet seen** ... prepared an ark for the salvation of his household*" (NASB). These and other works described in Hebrews 11 (such as Abraham offering up Isaac) are not themselves faith, but were motivated or empowered **by faith**. Therefore, they are called the "*work of faith*" (1 Thess. 1:3; 2 Thess. 1:11).

To be clear, faith itself is *not* a work as the Bible uses the term *work*. Faith is a matter of the heart, whereas a work is something done by the body. A work does something in the physical world that can be observed—like words that are spoken or an ark that has been built. More will be said about this in section 5.1, "Repentance Isn't a

---

[26] Those who do *not* believe all things written in the Bible have not believed in the God *of* the Bible. Instead, they are forming their notions of God and His Son from other sources (which implicitly say, "*This* thing which is written in the Bible **God** did not speak through the prophets and apostles and isn't true").

Work."

True Faith Will Produce Works

Nevertheless, James 2:14 and 20 teach us that true faith will produce works. No one will be saved with a faith which will not motivate "works of faith." God will not save those who have that kind of faith, nor can faith itself save them: Only God saves, and He saves only those with true faith.

But we should be clear on this point also: Those works of faith do not *make* faith acceptable. To the contrary, they are the result of, and therefore **evidence** of, true faith. Would you agree that a person must have such faith *before* they can do works *motivated by* that faith?

And God, who knows all hearts, needs no evidence to discern true faith. He saves those who have such faith, apart from their works, as it is written, "*To the one not working, but believing on Him justifying the ungodly, his faith is counted for righteousness ... God counts righteousness apart from works*" (Rom. 4:5–6 LITV).

Since acceptable or true faith will produce works, it must include something which will motivate and result in works. That "something" is **a mindset to trust** what you have believed because you are fully persuaded (Rom. 4:21) it is true. It is the mindset of the faith expressed in Psalm 91:2: "*He is my refuge and my fortress; my God, in Him I will trust.*" It motivates and results in *relying on* what you have believed, regardless of the perceived earthly consequences,[27] because you know that trust will ultimately be rewarded.

To illustrate, someone may say, "This investment will do better than

---

[27] As Jesus expressed in Luke 12:4, "*And I say to you, My friends, do not be afraid of those who kill the body, and after that have no more that they can do,*" and in Matt. 6:31-33, "*Therefore do not worry, saying, 'What shall we eat?' ... For your heavenly Father knows that you need all these things. But seek first the kingdom of God and His righteousness, and all these things shall be added to you.*"

all others," and you might say "I believe it!" But if someone listening to the conversation were to ask, perhaps with a chuckle, "Then, will you sell all of your other investments and buy this one?" and you were to answer, "Well, no," we would expect those in the conversation to think that you do not *truly* believe it. For true belief would impel you to rely on that belief—being fully persuaded that selling all of your other investments and buying that one would be generously rewarded.

That investment scenario is similar to the one-verse parable Jesus told in Matthew 13:44 about the kingdom of heaven: "*The kingdom of heaven is like a treasure hidden in the field, which a man found and hid again; and from joy over it he goes and sells all that he has and buys that field*" (NASB). The man sold all that he had to buy that field because 1) its price was all that he had, and 2) he was fully persuaded the treasure hidden in it was worth far more than all he had.

The man in the parable trusted, or relied on, what he truly believed *by* doing things (works) consistent with what he believed—he went and sold all that he had to buy that field. But the *mindset* to trust that belief, which was *part of* his true belief, and existed before and motivated his works, is not itself a work. Simply stated, true belief or faith is "trusting belief."

The Link between Faith and Repentance

These last attributes of true faith can be briefly summarized as follows: When those who truly believe in Jesus examine their personal faith (as directed by 2 Cor. 13:5), they should see that they believe whatever they understand Jesus has said and have a mindset to believe whatever they may come to understand He has said. They should also see that they have a mindset to trust in Him in whom they have believed—to rely on what He has said.

It may be easy to believe and rely on some things that someone might tell us. For example, someone we trust might tell us, "That Rocky Road ice cream is the best!" But to believe what Jesus has told us is a most severe test of one's personal faith in Him—for He has said that if we *desire* to save our life in this world, we will lose it eternally (John 12:25; Luke 9:24). One must *truly* believe in Jesus in order to receive those words of His. Indeed, one must trust Him above all else in this world—one must have no other lords before Him (Matt. 6:24).

Although true *faith* is different from a plain[28] *resolve* to do God's will (repentance), we can see now the intimate link between the two. The mindset to trust in Jesus, believing what He has said with a faith that is fully persuaded it is reliable, *impels* one to resolve to follow Him (to resolve to do God's will[29])—that is, to repent.

Because of this, true faith, and only true faith, will result in true repentance. One who truly believes in the Lord Jesus will repent and will call on Him and will be saved. This turning all hinges on faith. Hence, *"Believe in the Lord Jesus, and you will be saved"* (Acts 16:31 NASB).

3.2 True Faith and Repentance Come Together
The Ninevites' Faith and Repentance

Jesus told us in Luke 11:32 that *"men of Nineveh ... repented at the preaching of Jonah."* It is interesting to look at the account of Jonah's preaching to the Ninevites, since there is no mention of a need to believe in God or to repent, yet the Ninevites believed and repented. Also, there is no mention of good news in his preaching— of the possibility (let alone a promise) to be delivered from the consequences of their sins should they believe and repent. Jonah's preaching was only *bad news* for the Ninevites: *"Yet forty days, and Nineveh shall be overthrown"* (Jonah 3:4).

As Jonah went about Nineveh proclaiming this bad news, they surely asked him why he was saying these things. Who would overthrow their great city and why? In answering, he undoubtedly told them that he was *"a Hebrew"* who served *"the LORD, the God of heaven, who made the sea and the dry land"* (Jonah 1:9), and that God had

---

[28] "Plain" in the sense of unadulterated.
[29] God's will is, of course, expressed in what He has said to us in the Bible.

told him to "*cry out against it [Nineveh]; for their wickedness has come up before Me*" (Jonah 1:2). They may then have asked, "What terrible wickedness are we doing?" and, by contrast, what God's will is.

But then we are told that "*the people of Nineveh believed God*" (Jonah 3:5). In this context, that belief must have included believing that there is a God who made the world and all that is in it, and that because of the wickedness they were doing before Him, He was going to overthrow them.

Although there is no indication they were told of any possibility of escaping their fate, and Jonah did not want them to escape it (Jonah 3:10–4:1), they did what we would naturally expect their belief would impel them to do: Having no other recourse, and nothing to lose, they earnestly sought to find mercy from the One against whom they had sinned and who was going to destroy them. They turned from their evil ways, proclaimed a fast, and cried mightily to God (Jonah 3:5, 8). The king of Nineveh encouraged them to do so, saying, "**Who knows** *if He will turn ... from the heat of His anger and we will not perish?*" (Jonah 3:9 ATR) And the "*gracious and merciful God, [who is] slow to anger and abundant in lovingkindness*" (Jonah 4:2), had pity on them.

True Faith Is Necessary for Repentance

A passage in John demonstrates that true faith is necessary to support true repentance. John 6:51–61 records a teaching Jesus gave that a number of His disciples found hard and offensive. Consequently, many turned from following Jesus and, therefore, from repentance. As verse 66 describes, "*Many of His disciples went away into the things behind, and no longer walked with Him*" (LITV). Jesus then asked the twelve if they also wanted to go. Peter answered they did not, and gave as a reason, "*Lord, to whom shall we go? You have the Words of everlasting life. And we have believed and have known that You are the Christ, the Son of the living God*" (vv. 68–69 LITV).

Since Peter's answer gave a reason for continuing to follow Jesus, it should be assumed that those who went away did not have that reason (or they would have also continued to follow Him).[30] Peter expressed that because they knew (had truly believed) Jesus is the Son of God, the One who has the Words of eternal life, there was no other to whom they could or would go.

It is important to observe that Peter's reason had *nothing* to do with the specific teaching or some understanding of it that made it more acceptable to them. This reason would apply to *anything* Jesus might teach. Therefore, any of Jesus' teaching which they might otherwise find hard or offensive would not cause them to stop following Him. Instead, they would repent and turn from any such hard thoughts about His teaching and follow the One who alone is good—knowing, as the Scriptures say, *"There is a way which seems right to a man, but its end is the way of death"* (Prov. 16:25 NASB).

Their belief that Jesus is the Son of God was the **basis** for their repentance. Conversely, the disciples who left did not have that same faith that would support true repentance. Jesus, who *"knew from the beginning who they were"* (v. 64 LITV), bore witness of that problem before they went away when He said, *"But there are some of you who are not believing"* (v. 64 LITV). There were some who did not believe that Jesus spoke *"the Words of everlasting life,"* but they sat in judgment of what He said; and in this case, they judged His teaching to be offensive.

True Faith in Jesus Must Result in Repentance

Because of who Jesus is and what He has demanded, true faith in Him must result in repentance. For instance, Jesus said in Luke 13:5, *"Unless you repent you will all likewise perish."* Since Jesus made that statement, any *unrepentant* persons who claim to believe in

---

[30] Of course, some who had not truly believed might continue to follow Jesus anyway—just as the disciples who left had *"walked with Him"* before they left. In fact, that was the case here, as Jesus stated in v. 70 about Judas. Peter, unlike Jesus, could not know for certain the thoughts of the hearts of all the twelve, but answered from his heart and what he perceived about the others.

Jesus ought to believe they themselves will perish in their sins. The only alternative to believing they will perish in their unrepentance would be for them to claim, "Oh, I believe in **Jesus**, I just don't believe what He **said**."

However, Jesus explicitly rejected the kind of faith in Him that rejects the words He spoke when He said, "*The one who ... does not receive My Words has that judging him: the Word which I spoke, that will judge him in the last Day*" (John 12:48 LITV).

At the risk of stating the obvious, Jesus wants us to keep His commands. He said, "*If you love Me, keep My commandments*" (John 14:15). In the last verse in Matthew, in a passage that is commonly called "the Great Commission," Jesus said His disciples should teach new believers "*to observe all things that I have commanded you*" (Matt. 28:20). Accordingly, in John 15:14 He said, "*You are My friends if you do whatever I command you.*" When they hear Jesus' commands, those with true faith in Him *resolve* to keep them. That is, they are repentant.

True Faith and Repentance Always Come Together

True faith provides the basis for and results in true repentance. Therefore, true faith and repentance, although they are different things, always come together.[31]

That understanding led the apostles and Jewish Christians in Jerusalem, when they heard that Cornelius and other Gentiles had **believed** and been given the Holy Spirit (Acts 11:17; 10:43–44, 47), to **conclude** in Acts 11:18, "*Then God also has granted to the nations [the Gentiles] repentance unto life*" (LITV).[32] Note also that

---

[31] Of course, this relationship between true faith and true repentance in the New Testament does not necessarily exist between other kinds or definitions of faith and repentance—which may *not* come together, nor come in the same order. For example, a person who does not truly believe in God might repent from some sin.

[32] Cornelius could have understood that repentance is required to escape the judgment Peter spoke of in Acts 10:42 because, in v. 35, Peter told

just as Ephesians 2:8 says we are saved through faith, this passage in Acts shows that the repentance which always accompanies true faith is also necessary to be given life and be saved. For, it tells us, "God ... has granted ... repentance **unto life**." In like manner, 2 Corinthians 7:10 shows that repentance is necessary to be saved when it says, "*The grief according to God works repentance **to** salvation*" (LITV).

A careful look at a passage in Acts 26:17–20 shows that repentance should be preached in the gospel, and that both faith and repentance are necessary to inherit eternal life. (These truths will be proved later in this chapter—in section 3.5, "Repentance Is Preached in the True Gospel," and section 3.4, "The Unrepentant Will Not Be Saved.")

In verses 17–18, Jesus charged Paul, "*I am sending you, to open their eyes so that they may turn from darkness to light and from the dominion of Satan to God, that they may receive forgiveness of sins and an inheritance among those who have been sanctified by faith in Me*" (NASB). "*Open their eyes*" in this passage means to enlighten their understanding through preaching the gospel so that they may receive the truth and believe in Jesus. The purpose of that is "*so that they may **turn** ... to God*." And the purpose of that turning is "*that they may receive **forgiveness of sins** and **an inheritance among those** who have been sanctified by faith in Me*."

In verses 19–20, Paul then described his obedience to Jesus' charge,

---

Cornelius, "*The one **fearing Him** and **working righteousness** is acceptable to Him*" (LITV). This fear of God stands in contrast to **despising Him** by considering it unimportant to obey Him. It refers to a heart that fears to "work *un*righteousness"—that fears to willfully disobey Him. Before Peter came, Cornelius, having some belief in God, appeared to naturally understand that a repentant heart is necessary to be accepted by God—since he had been fearing God, fasting, praying, and giving alms (vv. 2, 4, and 30–31). The converse would be for a man to think that he could be accepted by God while in his heart he despises Him, sees no need to pray to Him, and oppresses the poor. Further, in v. 36, Peter described the position and authority which Jesus has, "*This One is Lord of all*" (LITV). It is only right to seek to obey the One who has that singular position and authority over you and all things.

*"I was not disobedient to the heavenly vision, but to those first in Damascus, and Jerusalem, and to all the country of Judea, and to the nations, I proclaimed the command to **repent** and to **turn** to God, doing works worthy of repentance"* (LITV).

The expression in verse 18 that describes what Jesus sent Paul to do—to open people's eyes so that they may *"**turn** from darkness to light and from the dominion of Satan **to God**"*—was obediently carried out by Paul through his preaching that included *"the command to **repent** and to **turn** to God"* (v. 20). This indicates that in verse 18, repenting is described as turning from darkness to light, from the dominion of Satan to God. Then, we can understand verses 17–18 to be saying, *"I am sending you, to open their eyes **so that** they **may** ... [repent], **that** they **may** receive forgiveness of sins."* [33]

Note that there are no "degrees" in the description of this repentance. It is not to turn from "darkness to duskiness," nor to replace some of Satan's dominion with God's. It is to turn to light and to God. (That will be shown thoroughly in section 4.4, "With the Whole Heart.")

Those who have a faith that leads to repentance have a faith that sanctifies. And observe that verse 18 describes those who are saved (that is, those who *"receive forgiveness of sins and an inheritance"*) as *"those who have been sanctified by faith in"* Jesus.

In addition to the *"command to repent"* that Paul proclaimed to all (v. 20), so that *"they may receive forgiveness of sins"* (v. 18), we are told in verse 20 that he also proclaimed we should be *"doing works worthy of repentance."* But be clear that this passage does *not* say those works are something we must do in order for God to forgive our sins and save us. And that includes the "work" of being baptized. [34]

The fact that we do not need to do works in order for God to forgive

---

[33] As we saw earlier, John the Baptist preached *"repentance for the forgiveness of sins"* (Mark 1:4 NASB).
[34] Otherwise, Paul's statement in 1 Cor. 1:17 that *"Christ did not send me to baptize, but to preach the gospel"* would be quite puzzling.

our sins is demonstrated well by the account in Acts 10 in which Peter preached the gospel to Cornelius and his relatives and close friends. In verses 44 and 47, we see that Peter had not even finished preaching when Cornelius, and all those with him who were hearing, received the Holy Spirit and were saved—having believed and repented in their hearts. More will be said about this in section 5.1.

3.3 Faith and Repentance in Salvation

The ordering of each of the four Gospels, together with a special emphasis each of them has, presents the gospel in a simple way, and illustrates the relationship between faith and repentance in salvation:

1. [The problem] **Matthew** especially convinces us of our sins and condemnation. For example, see Matthew 5:20–22. That was the sum of Jonah's preaching to Nineveh, and it can rouse someone's interest in the gospel. Further, Jesus came to call only those who understand they are sinners.

2. [Jesus is the solution] **Mark** especially shows Jesus' sole ability to forgive our sins and deliver us from any peril or distress. For example, see Mark 1:32–34 and 2:7, 10–11. (Note that Jesus is only able to forgive us because He, who never sinned, offered Himself a sacrifice for our sins when He was crucified;[35] and also, He was raised from the dead.[36])

3. [We must repent] **Luke**, being a physician (and physicians generally tell people what to do to get better), especially describes how to come to Jesus so that He will forgive us—which is in repentance. For example, see Luke 9:23–24 and 14:25–33.

4. [Believe in Jesus] **John** especially helps us to believe in Jesus (John 20:30–31)—so that we will repent and come to Him (as described by Luke), who is able to save us (as shown by Mark), from our sins and condemnation (Matthew).

---

[35] See Heb. 7:27, 10:12, 1 Cor. 15:3, 1 Pet. 1:18–19, 2:22–24, 2 Cor. 5:21, and Col. 2:14.
[36] See Acts 4:10, 2:31–33, 36, 5:30–31, and Heb. 7:23–25.

Acts 28:27 (as also Matt. 13:15 together with John 12:39–40) de-scribes the sequence of hearing, believing, repenting/turning, and salvation: "*Lest they should ... hear with their ears, lest they should understand with their hearts [perceive it as true, believe] and turn [repent], so that I should heal them [save them]*." The surrounding context in John 12:37–41 makes explicit that those not doing these things are those who do not believe in Jesus.

Acts 11:21 also describes the sequence of believing leading to repenting/turning. In it, the Greek word for *turn* is the same Greek word used for *turn* in the quote from Acts 28:27: "*And a great number believing, they turned to the Lord*" (LITV).

Jesus "heals" (Acts 28:27; 1 Pet. 2:24) those who come to Him in faith and repentance. That healing is often referred to as being saved (Eph. 2:5, 8; Titus 3:5). It is important to know that salvation is a miraculous act of God and that those who are saved have been radically transformed. Not only has God forgiven their sins (Rom. 4:5–7), but He has also put His Holy Spirit in them to dwell in them (Rom. 8:9, 11; John 7:38–39; Gal. 3:2), they have passed from death to life (1 John 3:14; John 5:25; 20:31; Acts 11:18; Col. 2:13), and have been made new creations—Jesus' sheep (John 1:12; Acts 15:7–9; 2 Cor. 5:17; Gal. 6:15; John 3:3; Matt. 9:17; John 10:3–5). They are said to "have" eternal life (John 3:36; 5:24; 6:47; 1 John 3:15).

But Jesus' work in saving those who come to Him does not end there (Mark 13:13; Phil. 1:6; Ps. 23; Phil. 2:13; 1 Thess. 5:23–24). It is later, when Christ returns and the dead are raised to either eternal life or eternal punishment (Matt. 25:46; John 5:29; Rev. 20:15; Dan. 12:2), that they "inherit" eternal life and the kingdom of God (Matt. 19:29; Luke 18:29–30; Matt. 25:34; 1 Cor. 15:50).

3.4 The Unrepentant Will Not Be Saved
Many passages in the Scriptures show that the unrepentant will not be saved. We will look at some in this section, and others will naturally come up as we look at various aspects of repentance in following chapters. Two such verses we have seen previously are Luke 13:5, "*Unless you repent you will all likewise perish*," and 2

Peter 3:9, "*The Lord is ... not willing that **any** should perish but that **all** should come to repentance.*"

However, some readers may have difficulty considering what the Bible teaches about this issue (or others) because of their perceived experiences. For instance, someone may say, "But **I** was saved (or I know somebody who was) without repenting!" Should we sit in judgment of what the Scriptures teach based on our perceived experiences, or should we seek to understand what the Scriptures teach and then judge our experiences based on that understanding? Those who choose the former are establishing their personal beliefs on their perceived experiences. It is something we must each decide. This book examines only what the Bible teaches.

As observed in section 3.1, James 2:19 warns us that there is a faith in God which even the demons have—who believe that God is One, and tremble! Luke 4:41 shows that the demons knew Jesus was the Son of God, and many were "*crying out and saying, 'You are the Christ, the Son of God!'*" And we are told in Mark 1:34 that when Jesus cast out many demons, He did not allow them to speak "*because they knew who He was*" (NASB).

The kind of faith demons have, which says, "I *know* you are the Lord of heaven and earth, but I don't purpose to *do* what you have commanded," is not a faith that has led to repentance. No one will be saved through that faith. The person who says, "I truly believe in Jesus, but I am still unrepentant," has been deceived.

What Do You Expect?

We must repent from our sins in order to be forgiven. Jesus will not forgive the sins of those who purpose to willfully continue in sin. Expressed another way, we must want to be made well in order for Jesus to heal us.[37] Some might find this surprising. However, when we consider what God required in the Law to forgive someone's transgression of that Law, and also consider our own personal experiences, we should only expect it is necessary to repent to be

---

[37] It is interesting to see that implication in John 5:6.

forgiven and saved.[38]

For instance, Leviticus 6:2–7 describes what God required in the Law to forgive a man who stole from his neighbor. He had to confess what he did to his neighbor and make restitution—restoring the full value of what was taken plus one-fifth more: *"He shall make restitution for it in full and add to it one-fifth more. He shall give it to the one to whom it belongs"* (v. 5 NASB). Then he had to bring an unblemished ram to the priest to offer for a guilt offering: *"Then he shall bring to the priest his guilt offering to the L*ORD*, a ram without defect from the flock ... and the priest shall make atonement for him before the L*ORD*, and he will be forgiven"* (vv. 6–7 NASB). If, believing in God, he wanted to be forgiven his thefts, it would quickly become apparent he needed to repent from stealing. It was simply impractical to be a forgiven, unrepentant thief!

Our personal experience should also make us expect we need to repent to be forgiven our sins. We would never expect to ask for and receive forgiveness from another person to whom we have repeatedly done some grievous evil *while* it is understood we plan to continue doing it. We would never expect to be able to restore a close relationship with someone that way. Jesus taught us that if our brother has sinned against us, *"if he repents, forgive him"* (Luke 17:3).

---

[38] Of course, this is different from proving what is taught in the Bible. And some things that are taught in the Bible are indeed unexpected. Nevertheless, God often uses our natural, personal experiences in this world He has created to help us better understand spiritual truths taught in the Bible. For example, in Mal. 1:7, the priests expressed their wrong notion that their defective offerings should be acceptable to God, saying, *"In what way have we defiled You?"* In answering, God did not tell them only the facts of what was evil about their offerings. He helped them to *perceive* that their offerings were evil by pointing out that their governor would not accept the same offerings from them: *"Is it not evil?* ***Offer it then to your governor!*** *Would he be pleased with you? Would he accept you favorably?"* (v. 8) However, we should be clear that God's morality is not at all judged or justified by a governor's morality. Their offerings to God would have been evil even if there were no human analogy and the governor would have been pleased with them.

Rather, what is unexpected (even astonishing) is that God would become a man and be crucified as a sacrifice for our sins so that He would be able to forgive those who believe in Him and repent from their sins (Rom. 3:23–26). Jacob expressed well the mindset we should have (despite *any* good thing we might think we have done) when he confessed, "*I am not worthy of the least of all the mercies and of all the truth which You have shown Your servant*" (Gen. 32:10).

Psalm 34:18 tells us, "*The LORD ... saves such as have a contrite spirit.*" As God says to us in Isaiah 57:15, "*For so says the high and lofty One ... His name is Holy: I dwell in the high and holy place, even with the contrite and humble of spirit; to make live the spirit of the humble and to make live the heart of the contrite ones*" (LITV).

Why the Unrepentant May Prosper

Many who are unrepentant find it hard to imagine their sins are not forgiven—that they are still under God's wrath and headed for judgment—given that things seem to be going well for them. They woke up today and the sun was shining. They had a good breakfast to eat, etc. Matthew 7:21–23 shows that many unrepentant people think even their spiritual lives are going well.

Asaph described in Psalm 73 how he also was misled for a time by the appearance that the unrepentant were prospering. He told us in Psalm 73:3–5, "*For I was envious of the boastful, when I saw the prosperity of the wicked. For there are no pangs in their death, but their strength is firm. They are not in trouble as other men, nor are they plagued like other men.*" That caused him to lament in verse 13, "*Surely I have cleansed my heart in vain, and washed my hands in innocence.*" But he came to his senses when he realized there is a fearful and eternal judgment awaiting them: "*Until I went into the sanctuary of God; then I understood their end. ... Oh, how they are brought to desolation, as in a moment! They are utterly consumed with terrors*" (vv. 17, 19).

God is kind in this life to many who are under His wrath. But Romans 2:4 tells us that His kindness is meant to lead to repentance.

Those who are not led to repentance, but go on rebelling against God while enjoying His forbearance, are in effect **despising** His kindness: *"Or do you despise the riches of His kindness, and the forbearance and the long-suffering, not knowing that the kindness of God leads you to repentance?"* (LITV) In the next verse, we are warned that those who continue in unrepentance are storing up wrath for themselves for eternity: *"But because of your stubbornness and **unrepentant heart** you are **storing up** wrath for yourself in the day of wrath and revelation of the righteous judgment of God"* (NASB).

In Luke 16:19–31, Jesus described a man to whom God had given riches and enabled to live in luxury during his life on the earth, but is now being tormented in a flame in Hades after his death. We can be certain the man was not comforted when Abraham told him in verse 25 to *"remember that during your life you received your good things"* (NASB). In their ensuing conversation, the man told Abraham that he had five brothers who were still living on the earth, and he begged Abraham to send someone to *"warn them, so that they will not also come to this place of torment"* (v. 28 NASB). In verse 30, he showed that he knew his brothers needed to repent to be saved from coming to the same place of torment since the purpose of the warning he desired for them was so that *"they will **repent**"* (NASB).

The Unrepentant Will Perish in Their Sins

In Acts 8:13–24, we read about a man named Simon who professed faith in Jesus, was baptized, and was thought to be a genuine, new believer. However, he showed that his heart was not right and he was still unrepentant because he thought that the gift of God could be purchased with money. Peter responded to him in verses 20–21, *"May your silver **perish with you** …You have no part or portion in this matter, for your **heart** is not right before God"* (NASB). He told Simon how he could be forgiven in the next verse, saying: *"**Repent**, then, from this wickedness of yours, and petition God if perhaps you will be forgiven the thought of your heart"* (LITV). It was not possible for Simon to be forgiven and saved from perishing in his sins while he remained unrepentant.

Jesus' teaching in Luke 11:32 shows that the unrepentant will be condemned:[39] "*Men of Nineveh will rise up in the judgment with this generation and condemn it, for they repented at the preaching of Jonah; and indeed a greater than Jonah is here.*" In this verse, Jesus spoke of "*the judgment*" that will occur at the end of this age, when the dead will rise up out of their graves—including both those in Nineveh who had repented, and those He was speaking to who were unrepentant. He said that in that judgment, the Ninevites who had repented at Jonah's preaching will condemn those who did not repent at Jesus' preaching.

The Ninevites will "*condemn*" them in the sense that the different response they had—repenting—will show that the condemnation of those who did not repent is just. Since the Ninevites repented at Jonah's preaching, there is no excuse for those who do not repent at Jesus' preaching—the One "*greater than Jonah.*"

Be Not like Esau

We are warned in Hebrews 12:15–16 to be careful that no one be like Esau: "*looking carefully lest ... there be any fornicator or profane person like Esau, who for one morsel of food sold his birthright.*" And we are told in the next verse that Esau was rejected from inheriting the blessing because he was unrepentant: "*For you know that afterward, when he wanted to inherit the blessing, he was rejected, for he found no place for repentance, though he sought it diligently with tears.*"

It is instructive to look at what Esau did and how his unrepentance was manifested. It is also helpful to examine the description because

---

[39] Jesus gave the same teaching in Matt. 12:41, and the Greek words in that long verse there are letter for letter identical (all 126 characters) to those in Luke 11:32 in many Greek manuscripts. [In some Greek manuscripts, there is an insignificant difference in the word *Nineveh* in the verse in Luke.] However, the preceding and following verse in each place are different material: Matt. 12:40 is different material from that in Luke 11:31, and Matt. 12:42 is different from Luke 11:33. That these 126 letters are identical is striking, and is one of those gems hidden in the Scriptures which demonstrate God did indeed both choose and order all the words in the Bible.

some may be confused about what it means to seek repentance with tears yet find no place for it. When we do, we will see the context shows that it was the blessing, not repentance, which the unrepentant Esau sought with tears.

The event mentioned in Hebrews 12:16—that Esau sold his precious birthright to his brother Jacob for one morsel of food—is described in Genesis 25:29–34. By Esau's doing so, Genesis 25:34 tells us, "*Esau **despised** his birthright*." In the same way, fornicators and profane persons despise that which is valuable by defiling it. And if anything is gained by doing so, it is worldly, fleeting, or insignificant by comparison.

Just like Simon showed that he did not have a right heart, Esau did not have a right mindset to sell his birthright "*for one morsel of food*." He had the mindset of those "*whose end is destruction, whose god is their belly*" (Phil. 3:19). Proverbs 28:21 tells us that a man will transgress for a piece of bread. Today, a loaf of bread can be had for less than a couple dollars. Is your soul worth a few dollars? Nevertheless, our God is rich in mercy and ready to forgive all who, believing in Him, repent from serving the various appetites and lusts of their flesh, and turn to God.

The comment in Hebrews 12:17—that Esau was rejected from inheriting the blessing because he was unrepentant—is based on a subsequent event that is recorded two chapters later, in Genesis 27:1–40. In that event, Jacob deceived his father Isaac and took his brother Esau's blessing. Isaac explained that to Esau, saying, "*Your brother came with deceit and has taken away your blessing*" (v. 35).[40] The blessing which Esau wanted to inherit, and his father Isaac had wanted to give him, is different from the birthright Esau had previously sold to Jacob in the earlier account in Genesis 25. Esau made that difference clear when he replied to Isaac, "*He has supplanted me these **two** times. He took away my birthright, and now*

---

[40] It is interesting to observe that, just as Jacob deceived his father by substituting himself for his brother, Jacob's father-in-law later deceived Jacob by substituting Rachel's sister, Leah, for Rachel on their wedding night (Gen. 29:25).

look, he has taken away my blessing!" (Genesis 27:36)

This was an exceeding grief to Esau, and he pleaded with his father vehemently for a blessing (seeking it with tears), as their interchange is described in the span of five verses in Genesis 27:34–38:

> *When Esau heard the words of his father, he cried with an* **exceedingly great** *and* **bitter cry***, and said to his father, "Bless me—me also, O my father!" ... "Have you not reserved a blessing for me?" ... "Have you only one blessing, my father? Bless me—me also, O my father!" And Esau* **lifted up his voice and wept***.*

Esau pleaded with his father as if he thought Isaac could give him a blessing if he desired, and sought to convince him to do so. He said, "*Bless ... me also, O my father! ... Have you only one blessing, my father?*" However, any blessing that Isaac could give in truth to either of his sons would have to come from God. Lamentations 3:37 rhetorically asks, "*Who is he who speaks and it comes to pass, when the Lord has not commanded it?*" The answer, of course, is "no one."[41]

It was God who did not permit Isaac to give Esau a blessing Esau wanted, and He told us the reason He did not in the comment in Hebrews 12:17. It was because Esau had not repented from having sold his birthright for a meal: "*[Esau, who for one morsel of food sold his* **birthright***.] For you know that* **afterward***, when he wanted to inherit the* **blessing***, he was* **rejected***, for he found no place for repentance [he had not repented from selling his birthright], though he sought it [the blessing] diligently with tears.*"

We can see Esau had not repented from the mindset that led him to sell his birthright for a morsel of food, by his representation of how

---

[41] Also, when God has blessed someone, people cannot revoke His blessing. Balaam explained this to Balak in Numbers 23:20, "*When He has blessed, then I cannot revoke it*" (NASB). Accordingly, Isaac told Esau in Gen. 27:33, "*Before you came ... I have blessed him—and indeed he shall be blessed.*"

he **lost** his birthright in Genesis 27:36. Esau said, *"He [Jacob] took away my birthright, and now look, he has taken away my blessing!"* Esau could not have repented from having sold his birthright since he blamed Jacob for taking it (though he was well aware of the deal he willingly made and swore to). You cannot repent from what you deny.

Esau rejected the correction which the bitter consequences of his actions might have otherwise provided by blaming someone else. Therefore, Esau was still that same, profane man whose mindset had caused him to despise that which was precious. As a result, God would not then *give* him something that was precious. Esau could not inherit the blessing because he was unrepentant: *"When he wanted to inherit the blessing, he was **rejected**, **for** he found no place for repentance"* (Hebrews 12:17).

The Coming Judgment of the Unrepentant

Many Jewish people who were not bearing fruits in keeping with repentance thought they could escape the coming judgment because they were Abraham's biological children. Correcting that error, John rebuked the crowds who came out to be baptized by him, as Luke 3:7–9 records:

> *Who warned you to flee from the wrath to come? Therefore bear fruits in keeping with repentance, and do not begin to say to yourselves, "We have Abraham for our father," for I say to you that from these stones God is able to raise up children to Abraham. Indeed the axe is already laid at the root of the trees; so every tree that does not bear good fruit is cut down and thrown into the fire.* (NASB)

In the same way, many professing Christians who are not bearing fruits in keeping with repentance think they can escape the coming judgment because they "believe" in Jesus.

But no one will be accepted by Jesus who says, "I believe you are the Lord of heaven and earth—but I do not want you to rule over me!" Those who are not willing for Jesus to rule over them—who have not resolved to do whatever He commands them—are unrepentant. Jesus described in a parable in Luke 19 the justice He will dispense when He returns, and what the end of the unrepentant will be: "*Those not desiring me to reign over them, bring them here and execute them before me*" (v. 27 LITV).

3.5 Repentance Is Preached in the True Gospel

You may have heard someone object to a particular teaching by saying, "If people are taught *this*, it will lead to significant problems!" This is a very important crossroad: whether to understand what the Scriptures teach and conform one's beliefs to that truth, or to consider the expected, practical consequences of different teachings and choose what appears most profitable (as the chief priests, scribes, and elders did in Luke 20:5–7). I pray that you choose truth. Ultimately, believing or teaching a lie will not be profitable but harmful.

It is common for people to preach the gospel without mentioning repentance. You might have heard that the gospel *ought* to be preached with nothing said about repentance. However, in the true gospel, repentance is preached. How do we know? Because Jesus said it should be. After Jesus was raised from the dead, He told His apostles and those with them "*that repentance and remission of sins should be preached in His name to all nations*" (Luke 24:47).[42]

The word rendered *remission* is one we have seen rendered *forgiveness* in quotes from Acts 26:18 and Mark 1:4. This verse clearly implies that in the name of Jesus the good news should be preached that people can have their sins forgiven, and the hearers should understand that they must repent in order to be forgiven. In the Greek text that was used by the NASB translation, the need to repent to be forgiven is made explicit, because the word "*for*" replaces the word "*and*" from the Greek text used by the NKJV translation. In a similar phrase in Mark 1:4, both Greek texts have the word "*for*": "*repentance for the forgiveness of sins*" (NASB).

---

[42] *The Westminster Confession of Faith*, in chapter XV section I, says, "Repentance unto life … is to be preached by every minister of the Gospel, as well as that of faith in Christ." *Trinity Hymnal*, 680.

Regardless, we know from other verses that we must repent to be forgiven (for instance, two quoted later in this section are Acts 2:38 and 3:19). Similarly, in section 3.2, we saw that repentance is "*unto life*" and "*to salvation*" (Acts 11:18 and 2 Cor. 7:10 LITV).

Since we must repent to have our sins forgiven and to be saved, how could repentance *not* be preached in the gospel? It is only what we should expect. However, note that Jesus' directive certainly doesn't limit the preaching of repentance to the gospel, nor does it specify how or under what circumstances it should be included in a specific gospel message.

Much of what should be preached is *implied* by Jesus' directive. To be preached in His name, it must include preaching about Him. Also, the news that one's sins can be forgiven can only be received by those who understand they have sinned, and it can only be good news for them if they understand the benefits of having their sins forgiven (or the penalty if not forgiven). Of course, they will repent only if they *believe* the things that are preached, and in the One in whose name they are preached. The aim of the preaching is to persuade them of these things so that they may believe and repent—"*to **open their eyes** so that they may ... [repent], that they may receive forgiveness of sins*" (Acts 26:18 NASB).

Two verses from the gospel message Peter preached to Cornelius in Acts 10 show some of these additional aspects of what should be preached: "***He commanded us** to preach to the people [we are preaching in His name], and to testify that it is He who was ordained by God to be **Judge** of the living and the dead. To Him **all the prophets witness** that, through His name, whoever **believes in Him** will receive remission of sins*" (vv. 42–43).

Numerous books of the Bible describe the gospel, or aspects of it, or contain descriptions of what was preached (for example, 1 Cor. 15:1–7). The Scriptures were written both for the saved (2 Tim. 3:16–17) and for those unsaved who may be seeking God (2 Tim. 3:15). But Acts is the only book in which we have transcripts of gospel messages that were preached by the apostles to the unsaved after Jesus was raised from the dead. This is not to say those transcripts are complete. But of course their contents accurately show us some things that were preached in each of the messages, and they contain all the things God chose to be recorded for our instruction (2 Tim. 3:16). Those transcripts show that the apostles were not disobedient to Jesus' directive—they preached repentance!

The first of those transcripts is found in Acts 2:14–40. When the day of Pentecost was fulfilled, and the apostles were filled with the Holy Spirit, Peter preached the gospel to the crowd who had gathered. Interestingly, we do not find in that recorded preaching an explicit mention of the need to believe. But when the crowd, being pierced to their hearts by what they heard, asked Peter and the apostles, *"Brothers [and by addressing them this way, they indicated that they had received the things the apostles had spoken and wanted to be as them—their brothers], what shall we do?"* (v. 37 LITV) Peter answered, *"Repent, and each of you be baptized in the name of Jesus Christ for the forgiveness of your sins; and you will receive the gift of the Holy Spirit"* (v. 38 NASB).[43]

The next recorded preaching of the gospel is found in Acts 3:12–26. The occasion was the miraculous healing of a well-known lame man. Peter told the people who had gathered in amazement to see the healed man that he had been healed through faith in Jesus. However, here again, there is no explicit mention in what was recorded that *they* needed to believe to be saved from their sins. But in verse 19, Peter said, *"Therefore repent and return [the word for turn], so that your sins may be wiped away"* (NASB). And in the last verse of preaching recorded in this passage, Peter said, *"God raised up His Servant and sent Him to bless you by turning every one of you from your wicked ways"* (v. 26 NASB).

---

[43] If this were the only passage about baptism, and we did not have passages like Acts 10:47, 1 Cor. 1:17, 21, and Luke 23:43, we might incorrectly think that, in addition to repenting, we also need to be baptized by men in water in order to receive the Holy Spirit and be saved. Rather, the command to be baptized is given here as one of the first commands to those who have just believed in Jesus and profess to be repentant, as Matt. 28:19 and Acts 19:3, 5 also show. Therefore, being baptized is evidence of repentance and one of its first fruits.

It would not be surprising for someone to ask at this point, "Peter preached repentance to the Jews, but what did Paul preach to the Gentiles?" However, this question implies there were different gospels preached by the different apostles to different groups, which was not the case. There is only one gospel given by God (*"the gospel of God"*—Rom. 1:1; 2 Cor. 11:7; 1 Pet. 4:17) which all of His apostles faithfully preached. Indeed, we are soberly warned that **all** who preach are charged to preach that same gospel under penalty of bringing a curse upon themselves. As Paul said, *"But even if we, or an angel from heaven, preach any other gospel to you than what we have preached to you, let him be accursed"* (Gal. 1:8).

The passage in Acts 26:17–20 we looked at in section 3.2 makes clear that Jesus charged Paul to preach that the unsaved should repent in order to be forgiven their sins and inherit eternal life. In that passage, Paul said that he *"was **not disobedient** to the heavenly vision, but to those first in Damascus, and Jerusalem, and to all the country of Judea, and to the nations [the Gentiles], I proclaimed the command to **repent** and to **turn** to God"* (vv. 19-20 LITV).

As Paul said in Acts 20:21, he preached *"to both Jews and Greeks ... repentance toward God and faith in our Lord Jesus Christ"* (NASB).

It is not required that repentance be mentioned every time the gospel is preached. But whatever preachers would say their gospel is, and no matter how much truth there may be in that gospel, if it doesn't include repentance *because* they teach we **do not need** to repent to be forgiven and saved, do they not *"pervert the gospel of Christ"* (Gal. 1:7)?

Chapter 4

What Repentance Is

I have inclined my heart to perform Your statutes forever.
—Psalm 119:112

This chapter revisits the brief description of repentance given in section 2.6—providing more detail, proving it from the Scriptures, and expounding upon it. In doing so, some information from that section is repeated in this fuller description.

4.1 What It Means to Repent

Many correctly acknowledge repentance is required for God to forgive our sins and save us,[44] yet their description of the repentance that is required is different from the Bible's description. Some believe the required repentance can be simply coming to the understanding that you need to be saved. Others say that you need to acknowledge you are a sinner, or to agree with God you are a sinner. Many would add that you must feel sorrow or grief over your sins.

Jesus distinguished repentance from some understanding of one's sins when He said, "*I did not come to call the* **righteous**, *but* **sinners** *to* **repentance**" (Luke 5:32 LITV). Those who do not understand themselves to be sinners cannot be called to repentance—for they

---

[44] Be absolutely clear that it is **not** that faith and repentance *cause* our sins to be forgiven and save us, but rather that God forgives and saves those (and only those) who believe and repent.

will ask, "Repent from what?"[45] But it is implicit in Jesus' statement that those who understand they are sinners are not, thereby, repentant, but have need of repentance.

We ought to regret or grieve over our sins, and that grief can lead to repentance. But, as we will see in section 5.2, that grief is not repentance. This is shown by what Paul wrote in 2 Corinthians 7:9: "*I rejoice, not that you were grieved, but that you were grieved **to** repentance*" (LITV). Paul did not rejoice that they were grieved. But he rejoiced that their grief led to repentance. Neither of those facts would make sense if grief *is* repentance—each shows that grief is different from repentance.

In the New Testament, the Greek verb μετανοέω (Strong's #3340, transliterated here *metanoeo*) is used for *repent*. The noun form of that Greek verb, μετάνοια (Strong's #3341, transliterated here *metanoia*), is used for *repentance*. In the Old Testament, the Hebrew word נחם (Strong's #5162, transliterated here *nacham*) is used for *repent* (although that Hebrew word also has other meanings).

As the Bible uses the term, to repent is not to change how you feel about something you have done, or to feel differently about something you do. It is to change your purposes going forward. It is often described or referred to as *turning*—in the Old Testament with the Hebrew word שוב (Strong's #7725, transliterated here *shub*) and in the New Testament with the Greek word ἐπιστρέφω (Strong's #1994, transliterated here *epistrepho*).

Note that *turning* has to do with changing the **purposed direction** of your steps going forward, and not the steps themselves. It has to do with your **intended path**—the way in which you intend to walk and the desired destination of your walking. In the Old Testament, *repent* is used to refer to changing any purpose, whether or not a choice between good and evil is involved.

---

[45] Jesus expressed that truth in the previous verse when He said, "*Those who are well have no need of a physician.*"

Here is an example from the Old Testament in which the words *repent* and *turn* are used in relation to something God had purposed. God said in Jeremiah 4:28, "*I have **purposed** and I will **not repent**, nor will I **turn** back from it*" (LITV). This passage makes clear that by God's saying He would not repent, He meant that He would not turn from what He had purposed to do. He meant that He would not change His purposes.

But God *has* repented, or changed His purposes, at other times— though not because He is fickle or sinful. For example, in Jeremiah 18:9–10, our faithful and holy God described situations in which He would faithfully repent: "*And the instant I speak concerning a nation, and concerning a kingdom, to build and to plant it; if it does evil in My eye, not to obey My voice, then I will repent of the good which I had said to do good to it*" (LITV). That is, instead of continuing with His purposes to build and plant a nation, if it does not obey His voice, but instead does evil, He will change His purposes toward it.

The book of Jonah gives an account of an event in which both men and God repented. We previously looked at Jesus' statement in Luke 11:32 that men of Nineveh repented when Jonah preached to them. That repenting is described in Jonah 3:4–10, and there is still more that we can learn from it.

When Jonah entered Nineveh, he proclaimed what God had told him: In forty days, Nineveh would be overthrown. But when the people of Nineveh heard Jonah's preaching, we are told that they believed in God. And they fasted and put on sackcloth, from the greatest of them to the least of them. The king made a decree and proclaimed that "*each one **turn** from his evil way, and from the violence that is in their hands*" (v. 8 LITV). And he said, "*Who knows if **He** will **turn** and **God repent** and **turn** from the heat of His anger and we will not perish?*" (v. 9 ATR)

We are told in the next verse, "*And God saw their works, that **they turned** from their evil way, and **God repented** over the evil that He had said to do to them and did not do it*" (ATR). The Scriptures describe their action and God's reaction here using identical terms.

57

Because the people of Nineveh repented and turned from their evil way (which was seen by their changed works), God repented and turned from the evil (or harm) that He had purposed and declared He would bring on them.

Consistent with Jesus' use of *repent* in Luke 11:32 to describe only the Ninevites'—not God's—repenting, *repent* in the New Testament is *exclusively* used in the specific way we customarily think of it: to refer to turning from doing what is morally wrong to doing what is good, to turn to doing what God wants us to do. As described in the passage quoted from Acts 26, it is "*to turn to God*," "*to turn … from darkness to light*" (vv. 20, 18 LITV).

The following definitions are suggested for *repent* and *repentance* as they are used in the New Testament. The definitions are based on the Old Testament's usage meaning "changed purposes" or "turning." But they reflect the specific, narrow subset to which those changed purposes always refer in the New Testament:

> **In the New Testament, the verb *repent*—*metanoeo*—means to change your purposes to a resolve to do God's will.**
>
> **The noun *repentance*—*metanoia*—means changed purposes to a resolve to do God's will.**

The resolve of *repentance* is with respect to God's will in any matter, and therefore in every matter. In a small number of New Testament verses that use *repent*, what should be repented from or to is explicitly mentioned.[46] In all other cases, including every verse where *repent* is used as a command in the New Testament, it means to resolve to do God's will in every matter. The command to repent is a command to put oneself in, or restore oneself to, the state of being repentant. In the New Testament, a person either has or does not have repentance—they are either repentant or unrepentant.

---

[46] For example, Rev. 2:21 and 16:9.

These simple definitions fit well in every place those words are used in the New Testament. We will see in this and subsequent chapters that there are no passages or biblical doctrines that conflict with these meanings. The definitions are free of things which we will see from the Scriptures are *not* repentance (for instance, confession, remorse, faith, and things which are works). In the next chapter, we will also see that *metanoeo*'s etymology supports a definition that does not include elements of either emotion or works. A number of passages we have looked at, and many more we will look at, explicitly show that the resolve of repentance must be with respect to all areas of our life, and regardless of the earthly consequences.

Any suggested alternative definition(s) would need to meet the same kinds of criteria, as well as be consistent with the Bible's teaching that we need to repent in order for God to forgive our sins and save us.

4.2 The Nature of Repentance

The nature of repentance, as well as the need for it, is described in a number of passages in the New Testament which do not use the words repent or repentance. To look at an example, Jesus taught us in Luke 9:23–25:

> *If anyone wishes to come after Me, he must deny himself, and take up his cross daily and follow Me. For whoever wishes to save his life will lose it, but whoever loses his life for My sake, he is the one who will save it. For what is a man profited if he gains the whole world, and loses or forfeits himself?* (NASB)

Paradoxically, it is all those (*"whoever"*) who wish to save their life who will lose it, and those who lose their life who will save it. Jesus gave a similar teaching in John 12:25, in which He explained He was speaking about one's short **life in this world**, and whether one's life is lost or kept for **eternal life** afterward. Jesus said, *"He who loves his life will lose it, and he who hates his **life in this world** will keep it for **eternal life**."*

A man who *"wishes to save his life"* (or *"loves his life"*) is someone who is unwilling to part with some aspect of his life in this world which he understands is against God's will. He is someone who has not resolved to do God's will in every area of his life—but wishes to disobey Him in some areas. Then, according to the definition of New Testament repentance just given, "*whoever wishes to save his life*" is someone who is unrepentant. Therefore, Jesus taught in these two passages that the unrepentant "*will lose*" their life—they will not "*keep it for eternal life.*"

We will look at a number of other passages that show the nature of repentance without using the words repent or repentance. Often, they do that by warning us about our need to repent. They teach that those who do not want Jesus to rule over them will be condemned, those putting one hand to the plow and looking back are not fit for the kingdom of God, no one is able to serve two lords—we must have no other gods before God, those who do not forsake all that they have cannot be Jesus' disciples, and for those who go on sinning willfully there is a terrifying expectation of judgment. These all provide equivalent descriptions of what it means to be repentant in accordance with the simple definition given in section 4.1. They also show the ultimate need for repentance.

4.3 The Repentant Mindset
The repentant mindset, a resolve to keep God's commands and to do His will, is displayed and described throughout Psalm 119. The psalmist said in verse 30 "*I have **chosen** the way of truth*," and in verse 112, "*I have **inclined my heart** to perform Your statutes forever.*"

When you find yourself in some great trouble, there are two basic reactions you can have. One is to say, "By any means acceptable to me, I need to find a way to deliver myself that I think will have the best (or least bad) consequences." The other is to say, "Whatever I do, it must be according to God's will. For, come what may, my hope is in God's deliverance [while remembering that His greatest deliverance is eternal life]."

King Nebuchadnezzar told Shadrach, Meshach, and Abed-Nego that they would be thrown into a burning fiery furnace if they did not fall down and worship the image he had made. He challenged them by asking, "*And who is the god who will deliver you from my hands?*" (Dan. 3:15) But they answered him, "*Our God whom we serve is able to deliver us from the burning fiery furnace, and He will deliver us from your hand, O king. But if not, let it be known to you, O king, that we do not serve your gods, nor will we worship the gold image which you have set up*" (vv. 17–18).

In like manner, the psalmist expressed, "*My life is continually in my hand, yet I do not forget Your law. The wicked have laid a snare for me, yet I have not gone astray from Your precepts*" (Ps. 119:109–110 NASB). Hebrews 11:35 tells us, "*Others were tortured, not accepting deliverance, that they might obtain a better resurrection.*"

You may have heard it said that God's commands can be superseded by a higher precept that it is necessary to protect your life from danger, harm, or even the threat of harm. But the Scriptures do not say that. Instead, they teach that we should obey God's commands even when our lives are in danger—that is, regardless of the earthly consequences. Besides what was just quoted from Psalm 119:109–110, the psalmist said in verse 157, "*Many are my persecutors and my enemies, yet I do not turn from your testimonies.*" And Jesus said in Matthew 10:28, "*Do not fear those who kill the body but are unable to kill the soul; but rather fear Him who is able to destroy both soul and body in hell*" (NASB).

Accordingly, Revelation 12:10–11 tells us "*our brethren ... did not love their life even when faced with death*" (NASB; and compare with John 12:25). Paul expressed that mindset well when he said in Acts 20:23–24, "*The Holy Spirit testifies in every city, saying that chains and tribulations await me. But none of these things move me; nor do I count my life dear to myself, so that I may finish my race with joy.*"

Peter received the harshest rebuke of all the disciples when, after Jesus told His disciples that He must go to Jerusalem and suffer many things and be killed, Peter said that God would not let such a thing happen to Him. Jesus said to Peter in Matthew 16:23, "*Get behind Me, Satan! You are an offense to Me, for you are not mindful of the things of God, but the things of men.*" And two verses later, in words almost identical to Luke 9:24, He taught His disciples, "*For whoever desires to save his life will lose it, but whoever loses his life for My sake will find it.*"

When you read through Psalm 119, do you rejoice at the things the psalmist expressed? Does your heart say, "My brother!"? For the psalmist said in verse 74, "*Those who fear You will be glad when they see me, because I have hoped in your word.*" He had *placed* his hope in God's word *by* resolving to follow and to keep it. As he said later in verse 166, "*LORD, I hope for **Your** salvation, and [therefore] I do Your commandments.*"

None of us know all of God's commands perfectly. Therefore, those who have purposed to keep His commands have, by so doing, resolved to keep some commands which they do not yet know or fully understand. Those who are repentant—who truly purpose to do God's will in all things—want to know and understand better what God's will is. Otherwise, how can they do what they are purposing? Therefore, the repentant seek to understand God's will.

To illustrate, the psalmist asked God to teach him those commands that he had some ignorance of, and affirmed that, whatever they were, he would obey them: "***Teach me** the way of Your Statutes, and I will keep it to the end. **Make me understand** and I will keep Your Law, and observe it with the whole heart*" (Ps. 119:33–34 LITV).

4.4 With the Whole Heart

The writer of Psalm 119 expressed the repentance those have who come to God with an **undivided** heart—that is, their **whole** heart. In verses 145–146 he said, "*I have cried with my whole heart; answer me, LORD, I will keep Your statutes. I cried to You, save me, and I will keep Your testimonies*" (ATR). Notice that it is his repentant heart's resolve that is expressed in the language "*will keep.*" Conversely, Psalm 66:18 speaks of the case of coming to the Lord without one's whole heart, and the consequence: "*If I regard iniquity in my heart, the Lord will not hear.*"

In response to a man who said to Him, "*Lord, I will follow You, but let me first...*" (Luke 9:61), Jesus told us, "*No one putting his hand on the plow, and looking at the things behind, is fit for the kingdom of God*" (v. 62 LITV). Jesus was describing someone coming to Him with a heart that is **divided** by conflicting desires—part of his heart would like to plow, yet part of his heart is looking at the things that are behind him. And He warned us that "*no one*" with such a divided heart is fit for the kingdom of God.

Those who cry out to the Lord while regarding iniquity in their heart are coming to Him with a divided heart. Their heart would like the Lord's mercy, and perhaps is willing to obey a number of His commands, but at the same time there is some iniquity they are not willing to give up. That is, they are unrepentant. Their plea is in reality made with a clenched fist, as if saying, "Lord, I will not do this thing you have commanded, but save me, I plead." It should not be surprising that the Lord "*will not hear*" such a "clenched fist" prayer for salvation.

The Scriptures never portray that mindset as an acceptable way to come to Jesus and be saved. Rather, those with that mindset are "*those not desiring ... [Jesus] to reign over them*" (Luke 19:27 LITV; as discussed at the end of section 3.4, "The Unrepentant Will Not Be Saved"). It is the mindset of those who "*go on sinning willfully*" (Heb. 10:26 NASB; which will be examined later).

There must not be anything you value more than the Lord Jesus. For Jesus said in Matthew 6:24, "*No one is **able** to serve two lords; for either he will hate the one, and he will love the other; or he will cleave to the one, and he will despise the other*" (LITV). If you are *trying* to serve two lords, there will be times when the requests of your two lords *conflict*, and you will only be able to serve one of them. When that happens, you would be, in effect, despising the other lord. In other words, **we must have no other lords before the Lord Jesus**.

Significantly, that is the same thing expressed in the first of the Ten Commandments, "*You shall have no other gods before Me*" (Deut. 5:7). Therefore, we could word a requirement of the First Commandment this way: You shall be repentant. That repentance is a resolve to do God's will over the will of any other gods.

When Jesus saw that large crowds were coming to Him, as described in Luke 14:25–33, He turned and gave them many warnings. He warned in verse 28 to "*count the cost*" of coming to Him. And He plainly told us the cost in verse 33, saying, "*Whoever of you does not forsake all that he has cannot be My disciple.*"

This is the same thing Jesus taught about the kingdom of heaven in the two parables of the hidden treasure and the precious pearl in Matthew 13:44–46. In both, a man needed to sell all he had to obtain the desired prize. It is not that we have to dispose of all that we have, but rather that nothing we have can be more important to us than, or take priority over, following Jesus. Said another way, we need to come to Him with our whole heart.

Coming to Jesus with our whole heart means that we are willing to do or give up anything Jesus might require us to do or give up. We do not know what will be required of us to follow Jesus, but we have resolved it is worth the cost—whatever that may be. The cost such a one has counted is "*all that he has.*" That was demonstrated when Jesus literally asked a rich young ruler to sell all that he had. In that man's case, it exposed that he was not coming with his whole heart—and so he went away grieving, without the eternal life he sought:

> *A man ran up to Him and knelt before Him, and asked Him, "Good Teacher, what shall I do to inherit eternal life?" ... Looking at him, Jesus felt a love for him and said to him, "One thing you lack: go and sell all you possess and give to the poor, and you will have treasure in heaven; and come, follow Me." But at these words he was saddened, and he went away grieving, for he was one who owned much property.* (Mark 10:17, 21–22 NASB)

In Matthew 22:37, Jesus said that the first and great commandment in the Law is, "*You shall love the Lord your God with your whole heart, and with your whole soul, and with your whole mind*" (ATR). In that passage, Jesus quoted from Deuteronomy 6:5. The Hebrew word in Deuteronomy 6:5 that corresponds with the word rendered "*whole*" in Matthew 22:37 is the same word that the writer of Psalm 119 used six times when he spoke of his "*whole*" heart. Besides the passage previously quoted in this section (vv. 145–146), verse 69 is an example: "*I will keep Your precepts with my whole heart.*"

Loving God with your whole heart does not mean you do not love anyone or anything else. That is easily seen because Jesus said just two verses later in Matthew that the second greatest command in the Law is, "*You shall love your neighbor as yourself*" (Matt. 22:39). We have other loves and loyalties in our heart, but the Lord our God must be before and above them all. We must *resolve* that if or when those other attachments and devotions *conflict* with obeying God, we will deny them and obey the Lord. "*For this is the love of God, that we keep His commandments*" (1 John 5:3).

Loving Him with your whole heart does not mean you will have no *desires* in your heart to do something that is not His will. To give a "perfect" example, Jesus had a normal and healthy desire not to be crucified, and it was not sinful for Him to express that desire to His Father in prayer. But He also expressed His greater desire to do His Father's will, rather than His own, in Matthew 26:39.

If you have a child, you undoubtedly love your son or daughter. Abraham also loved "*his only begotten son [Isaac]*" (Heb. 11:17). But Jesus said in Matthew 10:37, "*He who loves son or daughter more than Me is not worthy of Me.*" God tested Abraham in this very thing, and Abraham showed that his love for God, and therefore his desire to do God's will, was greater than his love for his son.

Loving Jesus with your whole heart clearly does not mean you will never sin. But if you do love Him with your whole heart, then you have *purposed* in your heart, with a settled determination, *not to* sin. The writer of Psalm 119 expressed that kind of determination in verse 106, "*I have sworn and confirmed [a determined resolve!] that I will keep Your righteous judgments.*"

The Bible makes clear in both its teaching and examples that Jesus is the only person who has no sin. Like "*all the disciples,*" Peter expressed his determination to Jesus on the night He was betrayed that *"even if I have to **die** with You, I will **not** deny You!"* (Matt. 26:35) Sadly, we know Peter denied Him three times that same night. Nevertheless, it is generally believed from what is recorded in John 21:18–19 that Peter was later martyred because of his faithful testimony of our Lord Jesus.

Pharaoh is an example of someone who confessed his sin and expressed repentance, but had deceived himself about his heart's resolve. As background, recall that because Pharaoh would not send away the Israelites as God had commanded him through Moses, God brought many plagues on the land of Egypt. After one particular plague (a very grievous hail that killed all the men and livestock that were outside in the field, and broke the trees), *"Pharaoh sent and called for Moses and Aaron, and said to them, 'I have sinned this time. The LORD is righteous, and my people and I are wicked. Entreat the LORD, that there may be no more mighty thundering and hail, for it is enough. I will let you go, and you shall stay no longer'"* (Ex. 9:27–28).

Pharaoh was undoubtedly thinking at that time that he *would* finally let the Israelites go. However, God could see that Pharaoh was not calling on Him with his whole heart.[47] He told Pharaoh, through Moses, that He would make the hail cease at a specified time, so *"that you may **know** that **the earth is the LORD's**"* (v. 29). But He then also let Pharaoh know that He was not deceived by Pharaoh's words, as Moses said to him in the next verse: *"But as for you and your servants, I know that you will not yet fear the LORD God."* Accordingly, we are told that *"when Pharaoh saw that the rain, the hail, and the thunder had ceased, he sinned yet more; and **he hardened his heart**, he and his servants. ... neither would he let the children of Israel go"* (vv. 34–35).

Those who seek to do God's will may pray that God would show

---

[47] People may deceive others about what is in their heart, and they may even deceive themselves. But they cannot deceive the One before whom all things are naked and laid bare, as Heb. 4:13, 1 Sam. 16:7, Acts 1:24, 15:8, and John 2:23–25 tell us.

them if they are regarding any iniquity in their heart. It is a good, regular practice for those who are repentant. David prayed for this in Psalm 139:23–24, saying, "*Search me ... God, and know my heart; try me, and know my thoughts; and see if any wicked way is in me; and lead me in the way everlasting*" (LITV).

Chapter 5

What Repentance Is Not

Then Judas ... was remorseful and brought back the ... silver
... saying, "I have sinned."
—Matthew 27:3–4

Looking at what repentance is *not* can refine our understanding of
what it is. The passage at the top of this chapter shows us that Judas
was remorseful, confessed his sin, and attempted restitution. When
someone has sinned, those are often good and appropriate things.
However, we know that Judas was unrepentant (as will be discussed
later in this chapter). We need to understand that repenting is
different from those things so that we may rightly divide the Word of
Truth (as 2 Tim. 2:15 calls on us to do).

5.1 Repentance Isn't a Work
Although works result from true repentance, it is important to
understand that the Scriptures distinguish repentance from works. In
the New Testament, repentance is changed purposes to a resolve to
do God's will. A *resolve* is not a work (as the New Testament uses
the term *work*). It is a matter of the heart[48] and will. Similarly, faith
is a matter of the heart,[49] and not a work.[50]

---

[48] See, for example, Rom. 2:5, Ps. 139:23–24, 119:112, and 66:18 (all previously quoted).
[49] *"For with the heart one believes"* (Rom. 10:10).
[50] Rom. 4:5-6 shows this: *"To the one **not working, but believing** ..., his*
faith** is counted for righteousness ... God counts righteousness **apart from

A work changes something in the physical world and, therefore, can be observed. Accordingly, James 2:18 describes unobservable faith being shown by observable works which that faith motivates: "*I will show you my faith by my works [that my faith motivates]*." Whatever else we learn from Philippians 2:13, the phrase in it, "*both to will and to work*" (NASB), shows that, biblically, "*to will*" is something different from "*to work*."

This difference between repentance and works is also shown in Acts 26:20. In it, Paul summarized for King Agrippa what he preached to all: that they should "*repent and to turn to God, doing works worthy of repentance*" (LITV). This statement does not talk about "doing the works that are repentance." It distinguishes repentance from works by talking about doing works that are worthy of, or befitting, repentance.

When someone has truly changed their purposes, that will affect their actions or works. If someone behaves no differently after they have changed their purposes as they would have behaved before, how can it be said they have changed their purposes? The result and evidence of changed purposes will be changed works. The Bible often refers to those changed works that are the result of repentance as the "*fruits*" of repentance.

John the Baptist's interchange with the crowds that went out to be baptized by him shows that repentance and works are different. John came preaching a baptism of repentance for the forgiveness of sins. Those coming to a baptism of repentance are professing repentance. But when John saw that the *crowds* were coming to him to be baptized, he said to them in Luke 3:7–8, "*Brood of vipers, who warned you to flee from the wrath to come? Therefore bear fruits in keeping with [the] repentance [you are professing]*" (NASB). The crowds were not doing the works that are in keeping with true repentance—the works which are the fruits that repentance bears.

---

works" (LITV). Gal. 2:16 distinguishes "*faith in Christ*" from "*the works of the law*," as Gal. 3:2 also distinguishes "*the works of the law*" from "*the hearing of faith*."

The crowds understood what John meant because they asked in response in verse 10, "*What shall we do then?*" Accordingly, John answered in part, "*He who has two tunics, let him give to him who has none*" (v. 11).

Giving a tunic to someone who has none is a work, but repentance is not.

5.2 Repentance Isn't Regret

Notice, however, that John did *not* reprove those who were coming to his baptism of repentance for *inadequately grieving* over sins they had committed in the past. For example, he gave no reproof for not properly grieving over having left a man without a tunic when they had an extra.[51] This is especially noteworthy, since here we have particular instruction about what was inconsistent with their professions of repentance. Similarly of note, even though Psalm 119 expresses the psalmist's repentant mindset throughout its 176 verses, his grief over his past sins is essentially unmentioned.

Although grief, regret, or remorse over sins that have been committed may bring someone to repent, and ought to accompany repentance, it is important to distinguish those *emotions* from what the New Testament means by *repentance*. Paul wrote in 2 Corinthians 7:9, "*I rejoice, not that you were grieved, but that you were grieved* **to** *repentance*" (LITV). Here, repentance is said to be a result of their grief and, therefore, is different from that grief. Also, grief is not something to rejoice over, but repentance is. Paul did not rejoice that they were grieved. But he rejoiced that their grief led to repentance.

---

[51] Even *not* doing something that someone knows to be God's will is sin, for James 4:17 says, "*Anyone knowing to do good, and not doing it, it is sin to him*" (LITV). In Luke 12:47, Jesus taught that knowing God's will but not doing it is sin when He said, "*That slave knowing the will of his Lord, and not ... doing according to His will, will be beaten with many stripes*" (LITV). This is as 1 John 5:17 tells us: "*All unrighteousness is sin*." Therefore, a resolve to do God's will is equivalent in effect to a resolve not to sin. In a similar way, turning *from darkness* is different from turning *to light*, but in practice they are equivalent.

In the next verse we read, *"The grief according to God works repentance to salvation"* (LITV). Here again, this verse shows that grief is not itself repentance, since it does not say that "the grief according to God is repentance" but that it *"works repentance."*

God draws[52] people to Himself in many different ways and through many different kinds of experiences, and they come with differing prominent emotions. In a metaphor in John 10:3, Jesus told us that He calls His sheep *by name* and leads them out. Your name is something which calls you but not another. Normally, if you call out someone's name in a crowded room, that person will respond.

In Acts 9:1–8, we are told how our risen Lord called the Pharisee Saul of Tarsus to Himself. Saul was exceedingly zealous in his persecution of Jesus' followers, and *"breathing threats and murder against the disciples of the Lord"* (v. 1). Jesus appeared to Saul and called him out by name (*"Saul, Saul..."*), confronted him with this great sin, struck him with blindness, and said he should go into the city and he would be told what he must do. There, Saul fasted for three days without eating or drinking, and prayed earnestly (vv. 9, 11). We can be certain he was greatly distressed over the evil he had done in his unbelief (1 Tim. 1:13), and praying that God would have mercy on him—until God sent Ananias.[53]

By contrast, consider how a rich, chief tax-collector named Zaccheus came to Jesus. We are not told what the various reasons were that Zaccheus *"was seeking to see Jesus, who He is"* (Luke 19:3 LITV). But that verse goes on to tell us that the crowd which was around Jesus was *preventing* Zaccheus from seeing who He is.[54] His personal determination to do so was shown by the undignified means he devised. Running ahead of the crowd, he left them behind and climbed up into a tree where Jesus was going to pass by.

---

[52] That God draws all those who come to His Son, see John 6:44 and Acts 16:14.

[53] Eating only after he was baptized, Acts 9:19 tells us.

[54] That situation could also occur today: The crowds that are "gathered around Jesus" for various reasons may actually hinder someone from seeing *who* Jesus is.

When Jesus came to the place, He looked up and saw Zaccheus in the tree. And Zaccheus beheld the Man who never sinned—who was sinless in His look, His bearing, His words, and His behavior. He looked into the eyes of the One who had created him, and knew all about him. Then Jesus spoke to him and *called him by his name*, saying, "*Zaccheus, hurry, come down, for today I must stay in your house*" (v. 5 LITV). And Zaccheus did hurry, and "*came down and welcomed Him, rejoicing*" (v. 6 LITV).

In contrast with the Pharisee Saul, who clearly came full of remorse and fear, the sinful Zaccheus came to Jesus rejoicing. And when the crowd murmured that Jesus was going to stay with a sinful man, Zaccheus showed his repentance by publicly volunteering, "*Behold, Lord, half of my possessions I will give to the poor, and if I have defrauded anyone of anything, I will give back four times as much*" (v. 8 NASB).[55] Whereupon Jesus said, "*Today salvation has come to this house ... for the Son of Man has come to seek and to save that which was lost*" (vv. 9–10).

Examining the Greek roots of words used for *repent* and *regret* in the New Testament provides some insight into the difference in their meanings.[56] The Greek word used for *repent, metanoeo*, is a compound verb formed from two words meaning *after* (Strong's #3326) and *to exercise the mind* or *to understand* (νοιέω, Strong's #3539, transliterated here *noieo*). From these component parts, we

---

[55] Although Zaccheus came rejoicing, we can see at the same time that he was ashamed of his previous deeds. Rom. 6:21 shows that Christians are ashamed of things they have done before they were saved, speaking about "*the things of which you are now ashamed*" (NASB).

[56] Note well that the meaning of a word as it is used in the New Testament is not necessarily determined by its root(s) or etymology. To wrongly assume so is known as the "root fallacy." See D.A. Carson's description of the root fallacy in his book *Exegetical Fallacies*, 2nd ed. (Grand Rapids, MI: Baker Academic, 1996, ISBN 978-0-8010-2086-5), 28–33. Although knowing a word's etymology may help us understand its meaning, a definition based on a word's etymology must be tested by examining how the word is used in its various contexts. Likewise, definitions of a word from different Greek dictionaries (which may even be inconsistent with one another) should be tested by examining the word's actual use.

can see a basis for its meaning: the "after" "exercise of one's mind" is distinguished from that before (in time). That implies changing the exercise of one's mind, or changing one's *mindset*. A good dictionary definition of *mindset* is, "A fixed mental attitude or disposition that predetermines a person's responses to and interpretations of situations."[57]

An example of a mindset is "a resolve to do God's will." The New Testament exclusively uses the word *repent* to refer to changing to that specific mindset—to a resolve to do God's will. And it exclusively uses the noun *repentance* to refer to that mindset. Consistent with the meaning of *repentance* in the New Testament, *noieo* and its related noun (νοῦς, Strong's #3563, transliterated here *nous*) never refer to or include either emotions or actions (works)[58] in the New Testament.

A Greek word used for *regret* in the New Testament is μεταμέλλομαι (Strong's #3338, transliterated here *metamellomai*). It is also a compound verb, and is formed from the same word that means *after* together with a different word meaning *care* (Strong's #3199). From these component parts, we can see a basis for its meaning: the "after" "care" is distinguished from that before. That implies changing one's feelings about something.

Both Strong's *Dictionary of the Greek Testament*[59] and *The New Englishman's Greek Concordance and Lexicon*[60] identically define *metamellomai* as "to care afterwards; i.e., regret." In its first definition of *metamellomai*, *The New Analytical Greek Lexicon* allows that it may express a change in one's feelings about

---

[57] *American Heritage® Dictionary of the English Language*, 5th ed. (2011). Retrieved August 13, 2022, from https://www.thefreedictionary.com/mindset

[58] One's mindset or understanding *affects* one's actions, and that is indicated in several passages in which *nous* appears (for example, Rom. 1:28, 1 Cor. 14:19, and Eph. 4:17). However, what one thinks with the mind (*nous*) and does with the body are clearly distinguished in Rom. 7:25.

[59] Strong, *Dictionary of the Greek Testament*, 47.

[60] Wigram-Green, *The New Englishman's Greek Concordance and Lexicon* (Peabody, MA: Hendrickson Publishers, 1982), 560.

something that does not include grief: "to change one's judgment on past points of conduct."[61] The New Testament's use of this Greek word is limited to refer to changing one's feelings or judgment about something specific that has been done.

Whereas the word for *repent* is always used in the New Testament to refer to **turning** from what is morally evil to what is morally good (that is, to a resolve to do God's will), *metamellomai* is used in the New Testament to refer to changing one's **feelings** about something **whether or not** it was morally wrong.[62]

Metamellomai is to **look back** on something that has been done with changed feelings about it, whereas *metanoeo* is to change one's mindset **going forward** to a resolve to do God's will. Unlike *metanoeo*, *metamellomai* is never used in the imperative in the New Testament (as a command).

Unhappily, some otherwise good translations have at times rendered both of these different Greek words as the English word *repent*. For example, the King James Version always did so (though the New King James Version corrected them all). That has made the specific meanings and different uses of these two Greek words in the New Testament less apparent.

Metamellomai is the word used to describe Judas' remorse over his sin of betraying Jesus in Matthew 27:3–4: "*Then Judas, His*

---

[61] Wesley J. Perschbacher, *The New Analytical Greek Lexicon* (Peabody, MA: Hendrickson Publishers, 2001, ISBN 0-943575-33-8), 273.

[62] Heb. 7:21 quotes Ps. 110:4 from the Old Testament. It is interesting to see something unexpected that was done there in the New Testament's Greek rendering of that quote from the Old Testament. The Hebrew word *nacham* for *repent* is rendered with the Greek word *metamellomai* instead of the Greek word *metanoeo*. In the following English translation of that part of Heb. 7:21, *metamellomai* has been rendered "care to change": "*The Lord swore, and will not care to change...*" (LITV). By using *metamellomai*, the more specific use and meaning of *repent* in the New Testament (*metanoeo*) compared with the Old Testament (*nacham*) was maintained. (Said more accurately, the different meanings of *metanoeo* and *nacham* were maintained.)

betrayer, seeing that He had been condemned, was **remorseful** *[metamellomai (inflected)] and* **brought back** *the thirty pieces of silver to the chief priests and elders,* **saying,** *'I have sinned by betraying innocent blood'.*" Truly, Judas' feelings about betraying Jesus had changed. He could no longer bear to keep the reward for his betrayal—the pieces of silver that had seemed so dear to him before.

Although Judas was genuinely grieved over what he had done, and so much so that we are told in the next verse "*he went away and hanged himself*" (NASB), that remorse did not lead him to repent. Even though he **understood** he had sinned and **confessed** it, attempted **restitution**, and in the end did the extreme "**penance**"[63] of killing himself, he was not repentant.

Sadly, Judas' grief and remorse did not cause him to turn to God, from darkness to light, purposing to obey Him—to have his sins forgiven and to be saved. Rather, it drove him to a hopeless, tormenting despair that led him to choose death.

That was a choice which also grieved God, for we read in Ezekiel 33:11, "'*As I live,' says the Lord* GOD, *'I have no pleasure in the death of the wicked, but that the wicked* **turn** *from his way and live. Turn, turn from your evil ways! For why should you die?*'"

Second Corinthians 7:10 describes two very different kinds of grief that have two very different results: "*The grief according to God works repentance to salvation, not to be regretted. But the grief of the world works death*" (LITV). Judas' grief was the grief of the world, which works death. In his case, it also led to his literal physical death. But there is a grief which leads to repentance which leads to salvation. And that kind of regret is not to be regretted because of the wonderful results.

---

[63] In the sense of the second definition of *penance* in *Webster's New World Dictionary, Second College Edition* (Cleveland, OH: William Collins Publishers, 1980, ISBN 0-529-05324-1), 1050: "Any voluntary act of reparation, self-punishment, etc. to show repentance for a sin or wrongdoing."

5.3 Unacceptable Repentance

The Bible describes things we should do that are "*pleasing to God*" (Rom. 12:1–2, Phil. 4:18 LITV) or "*good and **acceptable** in the sight of God*" (1 Tim. 2:3). Conversely, we are warned against doing things in ways that are *not* acceptable to God. For instance, Jesus reproached the Pharisees for the *motivation* behind their works, saying to us in Matthew 23:5, "*All their works they do to be seen by men.*" Similarly, He warned us not to pray or do acts of mercy for the praise of men in Matthew 6:1–6. This section looks at what the Bible warns us would make someone's repentance unacceptable to God.

As we have seen, the Bible warns us what the nature of the resolve of repentance must be. We cannot wish to save our life in this world, but we must lose it for Jesus' sake. We cannot come to Him with a divided heart, putting one hand on the plow and looking back, but must come with our whole heart. Jesus exhorted us to count the cost, which is that we must forsake all to follow Him. He warned we are unable to serve two lords—we cannot love anyone or anything more than Jesus. We must be willing for Jesus to rule over us. In summary, true repentance is a resolve to do God's will in all things. Therefore, there is no spectrum or degree of true repentance in the New Testament. Someone either has that resolve, or does not have it.

However, there are **no** exhortations or warnings about a need to have the right kinds or quality of **feelings** behind repentance for it to be true and acceptable repentance before God. This is reflected in the definition of New Testament repentance given in section 4.1 as only a resolve. In order for one's *repentance* to be true and acceptable, there is no need for it to include the proper *sorrow*, or for enough of one's sins to be *properly hated*. There is also no warning in the Bible that certain motivations or **reasons** for repenting would make the **resolve** of true repentance unacceptable.

In an issue that is not about repentance itself, but the evidence of true repentance, we are charged to do works that are worthy of, or befitting, repentance. We read in Luke 3:7–8 that the crowds going out to John's baptism of repentance were rebuked as being a "*brood of vipers*" because they were not "*bear[ing] fruits in keeping with repentance*" (NASB). Likewise, the Pharisees coming to John's baptism of repentance were rebuked in Matthew 3:7–8 for not bringing forth fruits (works) that are worthy of repentance. Because the Pharisees were not doing works worthy of repentance, we are warned in Matthew 23:3, "*Do not do according to their [the scribes' and Pharisees'] works; for they say, and do not do.*"

It may be that the most basic and sure fruit that true repentance bears is a *striving* to do God's will.[64] For how can it be that one truly has a *resolve* to do something that one is not *trying* or seeking to do? The unobservable resolve to do something is shown by observable striving to do it.

When we examine our personal repentance to see whether we "*are in the faith*" (2 Cor. 13:5), we should see that we have a resolve to do all that we understand to be God's will. We should also see that we are seeking to do it.

---

[64] The word *striving* is used here to refer to trying earnestly to do God's will with a devoted and serious effort.

Chapter 6

Reasons to Repent

You have delivered my soul from death,
my eyes from tears, and my feet from falling.
—Psalm 116:8

The resolve of true repentance is with respect to even the most private thoughts[65] and actions. Its ultimate *basis* is true faith in God, before whom nothing is hidden. The ultimate **reason** to repent is because God has appointed a day of eternal judgment, as Paul described to the Athenians: "*God ... now commands all men everywhere to repent, **because** He has appointed a day on which He will judge the world in righteousness by the Man whom He has ordained*" (Acts 17:30–31).

Although being delivered from eternal judgment to inherit eternal life is the ultimate reason to repent, it is helpful to know that repenting also leads to many blessings in this life. Moses encouraged Israel with that reason for keeping God's commands in a verse quoted in section 2.1: "*So you shall keep His statutes and His commandments which I am giving you today, **that** it may go well with you and with your children after you*" (Deut. 4:40 NASB). First Peter 3:10–11 gives the same kind of encouragement when it tells those who would like to have a life they love and to see good days on this

---

[65] Isa. 55:7 shows that the resolve of repentance is also with respect to our thoughts: "*Let the wicked forsake his way, and the unrighteous man his **thoughts**; let him return [shub—**turn**] to the LORD, and He will have mercy on him; and to our God, for He will abundantly pardon.*"

earth, that they should turn from evil (that is, repent) and do good: "*For the one desiring to love life, and to see good days, let him ... turn aside from evil, and let him do good*" (LITV).

In Luke 18:28–30, Jesus heartens all who have repented, telling those who have left behind things that were dear to them in order to follow Him that they will both "*receive many times more in this present time, and in the age to come eternal life.*" Accordingly, the writer of Psalm 119, whose expressed repentance and determination to keep God's commands was quoted often in the chapter on "What Repentance Is," testified in Psalm 119:65, "*You have dealt well with Your servant*" (NASB). David challenged us to put his statement in Psalm 34:8 to the test: "*Oh, taste and see that the LORD is good; blessed is the man who trusts in Him!*" The words "*taste and see*" confirm that David's assertion is something which can be experienced in this life.

God is good, and all His ways and commands are good. Conversely, sin is harmful to us (and others, including those we love). Because God made us, He knows how we are made to function best.[66] Jesus promised those who are burdened in their life on this earth that if they come to Him, He will give them rest: "*Come to Me, all who are weary and heavy-laden, and I will give you rest*" (Matt. 11:28 NASB). Again, Jesus gave as a reason for taking His yoke upon us and learning from Him that our souls will find rest: "*Take My yoke upon you and learn from Me, for I am gentle and humble in heart, and you will find rest for your souls*" (Matt. 11:29 NASB).

Further, we are told that God "*has pleasure in the prosperity of His servant*" (Ps. 35:27). As the Lord said in Jeremiah 29:11, "*'For I know the plans that I have for you,' declares the LORD, 'plans for welfare and not for calamity to give you a future and a hope'*" (NASB).

As described in section 5.3, "Unacceptable Repentance," there are no

---

[66] For that reason, some have likened the Bible to an owner's manual. In that comparison, there is an analogy in the humorous expression, "When all else fails, read the instructions."

motivations or reasons for repenting that would make someone's *true* repentance unacceptable to God. However, we must be very careful not to *adulterate* the **resolve** of true repentance with **reasons** for repenting. For example, do not mistakenly think that a resolve **to** obtain a better life through keeping God's commands is true repentance.

As we have seen, paradoxically, those who are seeking first things for their lives in this world (that is, serving themselves—seeking to save their lives in this world) will lose their lives. But those who *forsake* their lives in this world to follow Jesus (that is, to obey Him above all other lords), will be *given* not only eternal life, but also their necessary food and clothing[67] as well as many blessings in this life.

We can see an example of this principle in the way God dealt with Solomon in 2 Chronicles 1. When He told Solomon to ask for something he would like God to give him, Solomon asked for wisdom and knowledge so that he would be able to rule God's people well. God answered Solomon:

> *Because this was in your heart, and you have not asked riches or wealth or honor or the life of your enemies, nor have you asked long life—but have asked wisdom and knowledge for yourself,* ***that*** *you may judge My people over whom* ***I*** *have made you king—wisdom and knowledge are granted to you;* ***and*** *I will give you riches and wealth and honor, such as* ***none of the kings have had*** *who were before you, nor shall any after you have the like.* (vv. 11– 12)

Because Solomon asked God for what would enable him to do the very important work God had given him, God also blessed him with an extreme of what the world seeks that he did not ask.

The unrepentant pursue many things in this world with the hope that obtaining them will give them fulfillment and contentment, joy and

---

[67] Jesus promised this in Matt. 6:31–33.

peace. They rarely (never?) find them. And in the day such a man dies, "*in that very day his plans perish*" (Ps. 146:4). God tells us, "*What the wicked fears will come upon him, but the desire of the righteous will be granted*" (Prov. 10:24 NASB). God also withholds peace from the wicked: "*But the wicked are like the driven sea, which cannot be quiet, and its waves cast up mire and dirt. There is no peace to the wicked, says my God*" (Isa. 57:20–21 LITV).

But the life of one following Jesus has purpose, fulfillment, contentment, joy, peace, and hope. Jesus said to His followers, "*I have spoken these things to you that My joy may abide in you, and your joy may be full*" (John 15:11 LITV), and, "*Peace I leave with you, My peace I give to you*" (John 14:27). The psalmist rejoiced, saying, "*Blessed is the people knowing the joyful sound; ... they shall walk in the light of Your face. They shall rejoice in Your name always*" (Ps. 89:15–16 LITV).

But beyond these, and *any* other specific earthly blessings, we are told that "*He who did not spare His own Son, but delivered Him up for us all*" (Rom. 8:32) works **everything** that happens in this life to those who love Him for their **good** (even afflictions and trials): "*God causes all things to work together for good to those who love God*" (Rom. 8:28 NASB).

The Lord has told those who have forsaken all to follow Him, that He will never forsake *them*: "*I will never leave you nor forsake you*" (Heb. 13:5). The person who repents can expect in time to say with the psalmist, "*Return [shub—**Turn**] to your rest, O my soul, for the LORD has dealt bountifully with you. For You have delivered my soul from death, my eyes from tears, and my feet from falling*" (Ps. 116:7–8).

Chapter 7

Continuing in Repentance

If we go on sinning willfully ... there no longer remains
a sacrifice for sins.
—Hebrews 10:26 NASB

In Luke 5:32, Jesus told us that He *came* to call sinners to repentance. Titus 2:14 expounds on that purpose when it tells us that Jesus "*gave Himself for us, **that** He might redeem us from every lawless deed and purify for Himself His own special people, zealous for good works.*" Second Corinthians 5:15 makes a similar statement: "*He died for all, **that** the living ones may live no more to themselves, but to the One having died for them and having been raised*" (LITV). Would you think Jesus is satisfied that His purpose is fulfilled in a sinner who is repentant for just a moment?

Nevertheless, many in our day are convinced that those who lose or abandon a previously expressed faith will still inherit eternal life, even if for all practical purposes they become unbelievers.[68] They see this as an *inescapable conclusion* from an understanding that we are saved through faith in Christ and not by works, together with an understanding that those who are saved will not lose their salvation. Or, even if it *were* possible for those who are saved to lose their

---

[68] Charles Stanley, who was twice elected president of the Southern Baptist Convention, wrote in his book *Eternal Security: Can You Be Sure?* (Nashville, TN: Oliver-Nelson Books, 1990, ISBN 978-0840790958), 93–94: "Even if a believer for all practical purposes becomes an unbeliever, his salvation is not in jeopardy ... believers who lose or abandon their faith will retain their salvation."

salvation, it couldn't be the case that after being saved apart from works we would be required to do works to stay saved.

Although there is truth in the above statements, we will see that the "inescapable conclusion" they appear to support is faulty, and there is a different understanding that is in harmony with all the Scriptures. This chapter will thoroughly examine the Bible's teaching on this matter and its related issues.

7.1 We Must Continue in Repentance

A fatal problem with the aforementioned conclusion is that you have to disregard a large number of New Testament commands, exhortations, and warnings. In order to enter that club, you have to check a significant part of your Bible at the door. But in any matter of faith and doctrine, we must be careful to believe and receive **all** that God has written to us in the Scriptures.[69]

An alluring consequence of this faulty conclusion is that **those who have been saved** can live however they want and be sure they are "eternally secure." That is, there is nothing they can believe or do that would prevent them from inheriting eternal life.[70] However, note that by definition this certain, eternal security can only be enjoyed by those who have **surely been saved**.

Therefore, the hoped-for assurance of eternal security provided by this conclusion is no surer than one's certainty of having been saved. But there are many passages that should trouble those who are certain they have been saved and are now Christ's *even though* they are willfully living according to the passions and desires of the flesh. One of them is Galatians 5:21, 24: "*I tell you beforehand, just as I also told you in time past, that those who practice such things will* ***not*** *inherit the kingdom of God. ...* ***those who are Christ's*** *have crucified the flesh with its passions and desires*."

---

[69] As shown by Luke 24:25, John 8:47, and 12:48, all quoted previously.

[70] Charles Stanley reasoned on p. 34 of *Eternal Security: Can You Be Sure?*, "Can God declare me 'guilty' after He has already declared me 'not guilty' [when I was saved]?"

Let no one deceive you with persuasive words that because of grace, or because those who are saved will not lose their salvation, you do not need to continue in repentance. As we will soon see, the Bible is clear: Those who think they were saved in the past but are not continuing in faith and repentance should have no sober hope of inheriting eternal life. We will also look at some issues and questions raised by that understanding.

Jesus said in Mark 13:13 that it is "*he who endures to the end [who] shall be saved.*" In this context, "*shall be saved*" refers to inheriting eternal life. Here are a handful of verses which show that those who come to Jesus in faith and repentance so that they may be saved, must continue in faith and repentance so that they may inherit eternal life and the kingdom of God. They need no explanation, so they are simply quoted. Keep in mind that since true faith and repentance always come together, to continue in either is to continue in both.

Jesus said in Revelation 2:10, "*Be faithful **until death**, and I will give you the crown of life*" (see also Matt. 10:22 and James 1:12).

First Corinthians 15:2 tells us, "*by which also [the gospel] you are saved, **if** you **hold fast that word which I preached to you** ["repentance toward God and faith in our Lord Jesus Christ" (Acts 20:21 NASB)]—unless you believed in vain.*"

Colossians 1:21–23 says something similar: "*And you, who once were alienated and enemies in your mind by wicked works, yet now He has reconciled in the body of His flesh through death, to present you holy, and blameless, and above reproach in His sight—**if indeed you continue in the faith**, grounded and steadfast, and are **not moved away from** the hope of **the gospel which you heard**.*"

As Revelation 21:7 says, "*The one **overcoming** will inherit all things*" (LITV).

Jesus taught that those who come to Him in true repentance— purposing to follow Him, whatever may come—need to renew that resolve daily. He said in Luke 9:23–24, "*If anyone wishes to come after Me, he must deny himself, and take up his cross **daily** and* *follow Me. For whoever wishes to save his life will lose it, but whoever loses his life for My sake, he is the one who will save it*" (NASB). Here, Jesus taught that following Him (which is the fruit of repentance) requires denying yourself and taking up your cross,[71] and said that is something we must do **daily**. The reason He gave for doing so ("*For...*") is that **any man** ("*whoever*") who does not **wish** to do so—that is, every man who is unrepentant—will lose his life. There is no exception here for a man who, hypothetically, **was** repentant in the past, but **no longer** wishes to take up his cross daily and follow Jesus.

In John 12:25, Jesus said something similar to Luke 9:23–24 that makes explicit what is implied in Luke—one's life is **eternally** lost or kept based on whether one continues in repentance in this world: "*He who loves his life will lose it, and he who hates his life in this world will keep it for eternal life.*"

If a man who believes in Jesus and wishes to come after Him realizes he has not continued in repentance, the three actions commanded by Jesus[72] in the passage from Luke are *the same* whether or not he also questions if he has *ever* truly repented. For Jesus said, "*If anyone wishes to come after Me, he must deny himself, and take up his cross daily and follow Me.*" In other words, he should repent, and continue in repentance, and bear fruits in keeping with repentance. For we have a God who desires to show mercy and who is "*ready to pardon, gracious and merciful*" (Neh. 9:17). As He said in Ezekiel 18:23, 30–32:

> "*Do I have any pleasure at all that the wicked should die?*" says the Lord GOD, "*and not that he should **turn from his ways and live**? ... **Repent, and turn from all your transgressions** ... Cast away from you **all** the transgressions which you have committed, and get yourselves a **new heart** and a new spirit. ... For I have no pleasure in the death of one who dies,*" says the Lord GOD. "*Therefore*

---

[71] As was quoted from Gal. 5:24, "*Those who are Christ's have crucified the flesh with its passions and desires.*"

[72] All three verbs are inflected as imperatives in the Greek.

turn and live!"

Although *continuing* in faith and repentance is something *we must do*, paradoxically, the Scriptures tell us that God not only *gives* faith and repentance, but also *maintains* them in those who are truly Jesus' disciples. The reason Peter's faith would not fail, and Peter would turn back to Jesus after denying Him, was because Jesus had prayed for him (Luke 22:32). Philippians 2:13 contains this precious promise to those whom Jesus has saved: *"God ... is at work in you, both to **will** [repentance] and to work for His good pleasure"* (NASB). More will be said about this in section 7.5.

7.2 What Would Happen

Hebrews 10:26–27 is one passage showing the *consequences* to those who have in the past professed faith in Christ if they do not continue in repentance. It warns that anyone who does not continue in repentance regarding any sin faces a terrifying expectation of judgment. To help understand it, note that all who are *willfully* continuing to sin in some way, as a pattern, are unrepentant; there is some behavior they are intentionally doing or not doing that they know is sinful, yet they do not repent from it and *resolve* to do God's will.

The passage says, *"If we **go on sinning willfully** after receiving the knowledge of the truth, there no longer remains a sacrifice for sins, but a terrifying expectation of judgment and the fury of a fire which will consume the adversaries"* (NASB). In it, the *"we"* this warning is directed to is made clear from the preceding verses 19–25. Of course it includes **the author**, and also includes those who are his *"brethren,"* *"us,"* and *"ourselves."* Those categories include all reading the passage who profess faith in Christ.

The **behavior** that is addressed in this passage is someone **going on sinning willfully**. As reflected in this English translation of the passage, the addressed behavior is not *committing a sin*, nor even *going on sinning*. The behavior is *"willfully"* going on sinning as a pattern—knowingly, purposely sinning. It does not refer to any specific number or kind of willful sins. It addresses the behavior of **not continuing in repentance** regarding any sin.

Therefore, it warns all who profess faith in Christ and have received the knowledge of the truth that *"if"* they do not continue in repentance, they face a terrifying expectation of judgment—specifically, *"the fury of a fire which will consume the adversaries."* That is, their expectation is not to inherit eternal life, but to be condemned with the adversaries of God.

No doubt some will raise the promises God has made in the same Scriptures that those whom He has saved He will keep faithful to the end. Therefore, they will say, this warning cannot be directed to the saved. Then, is this warning intended only for those who are deceived about their salvation, and those who are not deceived about their salvation can ignore it? By definition, those who are deceived are not aware they are deceived. It is a warning to all who profess to have come to Jesus in faith and repentance that, as Jesus taught in Luke 9:23–24, they need to be diligent to renew that repentance daily. And the great and fearful reason to do so is that if they were to leave off repentance, they would face the terrifying expectation of judgment.

A passage about ten verses later, in Hebrews 10:38–39, warns those who have truly believed that if *they* do not continue in faith, their soul will be destroyed: *"But My righteous one shall live by faith; and if he shrinks back, My soul has no pleasure in him. But we are not of those who shrink back to destruction, but of those who have faith to the preserving of the soul"* (NASB). The one to whom this warning is given is clear—it is one of God's righteous ones who is living by faith. And this passage tells us that *"if,"* hypothetically (whether or not it will actually happen), that one *were* to shrink back, his soul would be destroyed. It is only those who continue in faith who will have their souls preserved.

In order for these warnings to be truthfully given to all who profess faith in Christ—both those who are deceived and those who have been saved—it must be the case that if the hypothetical were to happen, and some who have been saved were to become unrepentant and unbelieving, they would not inherit eternal life. It is useful for the Scriptures to tell us what would happen in certain circumstances that will not actually happen. And there are other examples where

God has done this.

One place He did so is in Matthew 26:53. As background, Jesus told us in John 10:11, 14–15, and 17 that He is the Good Shepherd, and that He lays down His life for the sheep. But in verse 18, He went further and said, "*No one takes it [My life] from Me, but I lay it down from Myself. I have authority to lay it down, and I have authority to take it again. I received this commandment from My Father*" (LITV). Here, Jesus went beyond telling us that He was willing for people to take His life from Him for the sake of the sheep. Rather, He told us *no one* would take His life from Him *at all*. It is with *authority* that He would give His life for the sheep (to be crucified for our sins, so that we could be forgiven).[73]

For Jesus' statement to have been true (as we know it was), it seems He would have needed to be **able** to prevent people from crucifying Him if He were to choose to do so. However, it was *impossible* that He would **actually** do that. One reason that was impossible is because the Scriptures *said* the Christ would be rejected, betrayed, and killed—as Jesus described in Matthew 26:54, "*How then will the Scriptures be fulfilled, which say that it must happen this way?*" (NASB)[74]

We are told *how* Jesus would have been able to prevent people from crucifying Him in Matthew 26. In verse 47, we read that it was "*a great multitude with swords and clubs*" that came to seize Jesus. How could any man deliver himself from being taken to be crucified by such a great multitude (or a much larger one)? Jesus would only be able to do so if, in the hypothetical case, He were to call on His Father and ask Him to deliver Him from being crucified, then His Father would do it. And that is exactly what Jesus said He was able to do in verse 53: "*Or do you think that I am not able now to call on*

---

[73] And if it were not the case that it was of His own authority that He laid down His life, then how could it be true that **He offered Himself** a sacrifice (Heb. 7:27; 10:12) for the sheep?

[74] For example, see Mark 8:31, John 19:36–37, Luke 24:25–26, Ps. 22:1–18 [noting verses 7–8, 16, and 18], Isa. 53:3–12, Zech. 12:10, 13:7, Gen. 40:16–19, Isa. 49:16, Ps. 69:21, and 41:9.

My Father, and He will place beside Me more than twelve legions of angels?" (LITV)[75]

Likewise, it was certain that God would deliver His Son from every evil, yet Jesus needed to pray to His Father to deliver Him. And He prayed with strong crying and tears—as if He would not be heard and delivered if He did not earnestly pray. Consistently, the Scriptures tell us that it was because of that pleading that His Father heard Him and answered His prayers: *"who in the days of His flesh was offering both petitions and entreaties to Him being able to save Him from death, with strong crying and tears, and being heard from His godly fear"* (Heb. 5:7 LITV). We see examples of those prayers in Psalms 69:13–17, 29–33, 22:4–6, and 19–24.

Being diligent to continue in repentance is included in what Hebrews 4:11 means by exhorting Christians to *"be diligent to enter that rest, lest anyone fall according to the same example of disobedience,"* and in what Philippians 2:12 means by exhorting Christians to *"work out your salvation with fear and trembling"* (NASB). These exhortations are a means of keeping believers faithful so that they may inherit eternal life.

7.3 What About God's Promises?
Someone will object, "But God has *promised* believers will inherit eternal life. It sounds like you don't trust Him." The argument here is that because of God's promises, believers can set aside God's warnings and commands which are true, good, and a necessary means of keeping them faithful.

Jesus gave a short answer for someone trying to persuade us to set God's promises against His warnings and commands. He said in Matthew 4:7, *"It is written, 'You shall not put the LORD your God to*

---

[75] Though an army be ever so large and well equipped, we may suppose it no match for twelve legions of angels. But if one were, then we are told *"more than"* that number—to whatever was needed—His Father would have placed beside Him. Jesus would have been able to successfully make this request because (and only because) His Father gave Him authority over laying down His life (as John 10:18 tells us).

the test '" (NASB). We believe and rejoice in His promises. But those promises are made to those who believe in Him. And those who believe in Him receive His instruction.[76]

It appears paradoxical that God has promised believers will inherit eternal life, yet He requires them to endure faithfully to the end to inherit it. But said a different way, it is as we might expect. God has not promised eternal life to everyone. Nor has He promised it to all who merely believe *that* His promise of eternal life applies to them. He has promised eternal life to **those believing in the Son of God**.[77] He has said that those not believing in Him will be judged (John 3:18; 12:48; Rev. 21:8). That category includes those who **never believed** as well as those who **shrink back from believing** in Him (as Heb. 10:38–39 describes, as discussed in section 7.2).

A passage in Hebrews 6:11–20 is an example of the teaching that God has both promised believers will inherit eternal life yet warned they must endure faithfully to the end to inherit it. In it, we will see that God's promise encourages believers to endure faithfully and comforts them over what they have given up and the trials they will endure in this life as a result of following Jesus. A later passage in Hebrews has a simple summary of these things: *"Therefore do not cast away your **confidence**, which has great reward. For you have need of **endurance**, so that **after** you have done the will of God, you **may receive** the promise"* (Heb. 10:35–36).

The passage begins in Hebrews 6:11–12 by exhorting us to diligently maintain and work out our faith and patience to the end. For it is **through** faith and patience that we **inherit** the promises: *"And we desire that each one of you show the same diligence to the full*

---

[76] God rebukes those who **talk** of His covenant and His statutes, yet do not receive His instruction, saying in Ps. 50:16–17, *"But to the wicked God says: 'What right have you to declare My statutes, or **take My covenant in your mouth**, seeing you hate instruction and **cast My words behind you?**'"* As Ps. 25:14 says, *"The secret of the LORD is with those who fear Him, and He will show them His covenant."*

[77] Be well aware that, as described in section 3.1, the object of faith is not a promise or a doctrine. It is the resurrected Lord Jesus in whom we are to believe (John 3:16; 9:35–36; Acts 16:31; 1 John 5:13; Rom. 10:9).

*assurance of hope until the end, that you do not become sluggish, but imitate those who **through faith and patience inherit the promises**."* *Matthew Henry's Commentary on the Whole Bible*, written in the early 1700's, says of those we are urged to imitate in this passage, "The way by which they came to the inheritance was that of faith and patience. ... If we ever expect to inherit as they do, we must follow them in the way of faith and patience."[78]

The next verses give an example of someone we should imitate— Abraham. Verses 13–14 talk about the promise God made to Abraham in Genesis 22:16–18, and its *absolute certainty*, "*For when God made a promise to Abraham, because He could swear by no one greater, He swore by Himself, saying, 'Surely blessing I will bless you, and multiplying I will multiply you'.*" Then verse 15 describes **how** Abraham successfully obtained the promise, "*And so, **after he had patiently endured**, he obtained the promise.*"

The final verses of the passage describe believers as heirs of that promise, and God's good purposes toward them in confirming the promise with an oath:[79]

> *Thus God, determining to show more abundantly to the **heirs of promise** the immutability of His counsel, confirmed it by an oath, that by two immutable things, in which it is impossible for God to lie, **we might have strong consolation, who have fled for refuge** to lay hold of the hope set before us. This hope we have as **an anchor of the soul**, both **sure and steadfast**, and which enters the*

---

[78] *Matthew Henry's Commentary on the Whole Bible* ([Reprinted] Peabody, MA: Hendrickson Publishers, 1991, ISBN 0-943575-32-X), 2389.

[79] To see how believers are heirs of the promise that was sworn in Gen. 22, note that it had multiple parts ("*..., and ...*"), only some of which are quoted in Heb. 6:14. And they were not to Abraham only, but **also** to his Seed— who is **Christ** (Gen. 22:17–18; Gal. 3:16). That Seed, Christ, shall possess the gate of His enemies (Gen. 22:17 LITV; for instance, of death and Hades—Rev. 1:18; 1 Cor. 15:25–26, 54–55), and in the Christ **all** shall be blessed (Gen. 22:18; 1 Cor. 15:22—that is, it is only through Christ that one may have that blessing, and all those in Him shall). Therefore, all those who are of Christ are heirs of this sworn promise (Gal. 3:18, 29; Heb. 6:17).

> *Presence behind the veil, where the forerunner has entered*
> *for us, even Jesus...* (vv. 17–20)

Regarding this passage, *Matthew Henry's Commentary* asks us to observe that "God is [also] concerned for the **consolation** of believers" (emphasis added).[80] And taking up the language that this hope is "*an **anchor** of the soul, both sure and steadfast*," it makes the analogy, "Heaven is the harbour to which we sail. The temptations, persecutions, and afflictions that we encounter, are the winds and waves that threaten our shipwreck. ... [And this anchor] does not seek to fasten in the sands, but enters within the veil, and fixes there upon Christ."[81]

Later, in Hebrews 11:11, Sarah is given as an example for us of someone who was **empowered** by faith in God's promises so as to be able to obtain those promises: "*Also by faith Sarah herself **received power** for conceiving seed even beyond the time of age, and gave birth; **since** she deemed the One having promised to be faithful*" (LITV). Abraham is held up as a similar example in Romans 4:19–21, "*And being about a hundred years old, not weakening in faith, he did not consider his body to have died already, nor yet the death of Sarah's womb, and did not **stagger by unbelief** at the promise of God, but was **empowered** by faith, giving glory to God, and being fully persuaded that what He has promised, He is also able to do*" (LITV).

During the time God's people had a kingdom of this world, if He told them that He would give them victory over an enemy, they still needed to go to battle in order to obtain the promised victory. Through their faith in God and trust in His promise, they needed to strengthen themselves and be brave to take their lives in their hands and go out to the battle.

For example, when God gave His charge to Joshua, He promised in Joshua 1:5, "*No man shall be able to stand before you all the days of your life. As I was with Moses, so I will be with you. I will not fail*

---

[80] *Matthew Henry's Commentary on the Whole Bible*, 2390.
[81] Ibid.

you nor will I forsake you" (LITV). However, in the next four verses, He charged Joshua to be strong and brave three times, as well as not to be afraid a fourth time: "*Be strong and brave. For* **you** *shall cause this people to inherit the land which* **I swore** *to their fathers to give to them. Only be strong and very brave ... Have I not commanded you? Be strong and brave. Do not be afraid or discouraged, for Jehovah your God is with you in all places where you go*" (Josh. 1:6–7, 9 LITV).

Joshua needed to be strong and brave in order to go where God wanted him to go and do what He commanded him to do. If he were to flee before his enemies, God would *not* give him victory and enable him to inherit the land.

Soon after, as the people prepared to go in to take possession of the land God had promised to give them (Josh. 1:11), they told Joshua they would do everything he commanded them. But *they also* implored Joshua to be strong and brave, for they knew that was necessary for him to be able to lead them in the way God would have them go—so that they *would* obtain the promised land: "*We will do all that you command us; and we will go everywhere you shall send us. ... Surely Jehovah your God is with you, as He has been with Moses. Whoever rebels against your mouth, and will not listen to your commands in all that you say to him, he shall die. Only, be strong and brave*" (Josh. 1:16–18 LITV).

They urged him to be strong and brave because they did not want him to shrink back from doing God's will. For if he did shrink back from it, they would be doing the hard work of going wherever Joshua would send them and facing every enemy they would encounter, all for naught—with God confronting them as an adversary, instead of helping them as their God and friend.

7.4 The Repentant Believer's Striving and Confidence

We have seen from the Scriptures that believers must continue in faith and repentance to inherit eternal life. Now we will examine some passages which, besides showing the same, help us better understand the believer's mindset.

94

Because the repentant have resolved to do God's will, they strive to do it. That striving is not itself repentance, but it is a fruit of their repentance. As described in section 5.3, striving to obey God may be the most basic and sure fruit that true repentance bears. Therefore, when repentant believers understand one of God's commands is "*do not sin*" (1 Cor. 15:34 and 1 John 2:1 LITV), they strive to keep themselves from sinning. They do so not because any particular sins, or some number of them,[82] at any particular moment or over any specific period of time would jeopardize their salvation. They do so because they are repentant. If they were not striving to keep themselves from sinning, they would be unrepentant.

At the end of 1 Corinthians 9, Paul likened himself to someone running in a stadium to receive a prize, and said that in his race he was striving for an incorruptible crown.[83] In this analogy, beginning the race is like being saved, and crossing the finish line is like inheriting eternal life (receiving "*the crown of life*" (James 1:12; Rev. 2:10)). In verse 27 he said, "*But I discipline my body and make it my slave, so that, after I have preached to others, I myself will not be disqualified*" (NASB).

Here, Paul gave a reason for striving to bring his body into sub-jection to God's will. It is similar to the reason given to all believers in Hebrews 10:26–27 not to go on willfully sinning: **If** he were not striving to do so, **he** would face the expectation of not obtaining the incorruptible crown. In the analogy, his behavior in the race would **disqualify** him. A man who is not *seeking* to bring his body into subjection to God's will is not bearing a sure fruit of repentance. And the unrepentant will not receive the crown of life. But Paul was seeking to do so. Therefore, that impossibility would not happen ("*so that … I myself will not be disqualified*").

---

[82] Such as "*seventy times seven*" (Matt. 18:22).

[83] As 1 Cor. 9:24–26 says, "*Do you not know that those running in a sta-dium indeed all run, but one receives the prize? So run that you may obtain. But everyone striving [by definition] controls ["to exercise self-restraint," Strong, Dictionary of the Greek Testament, 25, #1467] himself in all things [related to his striving]. Then those truly that they may receive a corruptible crown, but we an incorruptible. So I run accordingly, as not uncertainly; so I fight, as not beating air*" (LITV).

Paul used the same Greek word rendered *disqualified* in the passage from 1 Corinthians 9 again in 2 Corinthians 13:5–6: "*Examine your-selves as to whether you are in the faith. Test yourselves. Do you not know yourselves, that Jesus Christ is in you?—unless indeed you are disqualified. But I trust that you will know that we are not disquali-fied.*" This passage makes explicit that those who are "*disqualified*" do not have Jesus Christ in them—that is, they are not in the faith, they are not saved. It also shows that Paul knew that he himself was not disqualified.

Believers' *confidence* that they will obtain God's promises and in-herit eternal life exists *together* with their *earnestness* to run the race in such a way that they may obtain and to heed His warnings so that they "*will not be disqualified.*"

This seemingly paradoxical combination can be likened to a frail man descending some long, steep stairs, holding fast to the railing. Upon seeing him, you ask (not scornfully as some might, but rather having a concern), "Are you afraid you will fall?" He answers and says, "No." But you press him on it and ask, "Then why are you holding so tightly to the railing?" Whereupon he explains, "Because I fear falling. A man I have faith in warned me to hold fast to the railing and promised that if I do, when I stumble I will never fall. Therefore, because I am holding fast to the railing, I don't have any fear that I will fall." His fear of **falling**, and desire never to fall, causes him to be careful to obey the warning of the one he has faith in. As a result, he does not fear that he **will fall**.

Paul warned believers that they need to be careful to keep themselves from falling in 1 Corinthians 10:11–12, "*And all these things happened to those as examples, and it was written for **our** warning [Paul's, and those he is writing to] ... So that he that thinks to stand [that is, someone who thinks he is saved, one of the "our" to whom this warning is given], let him **be careful** that he **not fall***" (LITV; see also 2 Pet. 1:10; 3:17). But then also, our faithful God gave us this wonderful promise in the very next verse: "*But God is faithful, who will not allow you to be tempted above what you are able. But with the temptation, He will also make the way out, so that you may be able to bear it*" (LITV).

Paradoxically, the Bible teaches that we need to strive so as to obtain[84]—that we may attain to the resurrection from the dead[85]—yet those who are saved can at the same time know they have been saved (1 John 5:13; 4:13; 3:14), and therefore have confidence they will inherit eternal life (Phil. 1:6; 2 Cor. 5:4–8; 2 Tim. 1:12; John 6:39–40; 10:28; 1 Thess. 5:23–24). Is that not how we saw in section 7.2 that our Lord Jesus prayed, as described in the Hebrews 5:7 passage and demonstrated in the example Psalms?[86]

7.5 The Saved Continue in Repentance

As described in section 3.3, "Faith and Repentance in Salvation," when people come to Jesus in faith and repentance, and He saves them, they have become new creations and His Holy Spirit dwells in them. In this chapter, we have seen that the Bible teaches that those who are saved must continue in faith and repentance in order to inherit eternal life. Accordingly, there are sober warnings that we be diligent to do so. Nevertheless, we will see here that a careful examination of the Scriptures shows the wonderful **actuality** that all those who have been saved **will** continue in repentance.

The *reason* this is the actuality is because the Good Shepherd will accomplish it in all who have fled to Him for refuge. Part of Jesus' work in saving us is keeping those whom He has saved faithful.

Some careful thought should convince us that this actuality could *only* be accomplished with *certainty* by Jesus. For, if it were to depend on human will alone, we would not expect *everyone* who is saved—without exception—to continue in repentance without fail!

---

[84] See the previous footnote.

[85] As Phil. 3:11–14 says: *"if, by any means, I may attain to the resurrection from the dead. Not that I have already attained, or am already perfected; but I press on, that I may lay hold of that for which Christ Jesus has also laid hold of me. Brethren, I do not count myself to have apprehended; but one thing I do, forgetting those things which are behind and reaching forward to those things which are ahead, I press toward the goal for the prize of the upward call of God in Christ Jesus."*

[86] The ability to know you are saved and have confidence you will inherit eternal life is often referred to as "assurance." Having mentioned it here, it is not a subject of this book so it will not be elaborated upon further.

In fact, if the Good Shepherd were struck, *none* of His sheep would continue faithfully—*all* would be scattered![87] It is the Good Shepherd's shepherding that keeps His sheep faithful. Jesus' sheep continue in faith and repentance, as they need to, because Jesus both enables them to and ensures that they do.

Jesus told us He will not lose any of His sheep in John 6:39 when He said, *"This is the will of the Father sending Me, that of all that He has given Me, **I shall not lose any of it**, but shall raise it up in the last day"* (LITV). Paul said in 2 Timothy 1:12, *"For I know whom I have believed and am persuaded that He is able to keep what I have committed to Him until that Day."*

First Thessalonians 5:23–24 tells of Jesus' faithful work through which He will not fail to keep His sheep to the day in which they will inherit eternal life: *"May your whole spirit and soul and body be kept blameless at the coming of our Lord Jesus Christ. Faithful is the One calling you, who also **will perform it**"* (LITV). As Philippians 1:6 also says, explicitly referring only to those in whom He has begun a good work (that is, to those whom He has saved), *"He who has begun a good work in you **will complete it** until the day of Jesus Christ."*

But we should not think that sheep do not need to go in the way their shepherd leads and guides them because somehow the shepherd will do it for them. In Psalm 23, David described many things the Lord does in shepherding His sheep, and said in verse 4, *"Your rod and Your staff, they comfort me."* The Lord's rod (His correction or discipline) and staff (His instruction) are means by which He guides His sheep in the way they should go. Of course, it is painful when He applies His rod.[88] But His sheep are comforted by seeing their Shepherd's steadfast determination to keep them from wandering away and perishing.

John 8 records a time when, as Jesus was teaching in the temple, *"many believed into Him. Then Jesus said to the Jews who had*

---

[87] See, for example, Mark 14:27 and Matt. 9:36.
[88] See, for example, Heb. 12:5, 11, and 1 Cor. 11:30–32.

*believed in Him, **If** you **continue** in My Word, you **are** truly My disciples*" (John 8:30–31 LITV). The events that unfolded shortly afterward show that Jesus had a special reason to give this warning and teaching to these new "believers." As Jesus' discussion with them progressed, we see that they immediately objected to His word (in v. 33). And by verse 48, they had cast off any semblance of believing in Him, saying, "*Do we not say well that You are a Samaritan and have a demon?*" (LITV)

In Jesus' statement in John 8:31, He made a distinction between *all* disciples[89]—such as those He was speaking to in that verse, or those in John 6:66 who eventually stopped following Him—and those who are "*truly*" His disciples. Any who profess faith in Jesus can be included in those who are *called* disciples (as John 8:30–31 shows that those who had just believed in Him were called disciples). However, under the New Covenant, those whom Jesus has not saved are not *truly* His disciples.

It is important to observe that Jesus said their *continuing* in the future would reveal what they *are* in the present. In order for people to *continue* in Jesus' word, they need to *maintain their resolve* to follow Jesus. Continuing in Jesus' word is not something that happens by accident—apart from someone purposing to do so! Said another way, in order for people to continue in Jesus' word, they need to continue in repentance.

The impression we get from Jesus' statement is that a *test* of whether someone is truly His disciple is whether one continues in His word— that those who are truly His disciples *will* continue in His word.[90] And there are a number of passages we will look at which plainly teach that all those who have been saved will continue in repentance.

Another way of expressing this truth is that whether one continues in repentance **exposes** whether one has been saved. Jesus illustrated this

---

[89] Or *Christians*, as Jesus' disciples later came to be called: "*And the disciples were first called Christians in Antioch*" (Acts 11:26).
[90] However, you may observe that the strict logic of Jesus' statement does not prove this.

truth in His first parable recorded in the New Testament, in Matthew 13:3–9, "*the parable of the sower*" (Matt. 13:18 NASB). A parallel account of the parable given in Luke 8:5–15 provides additional insight into its meaning.

As we might expect of the first parable in the New Testament, the parable and its interpretation are especially important. For Jesus indicated that if we do not understand this parable, we will have trouble understanding any of the parables.[91] Then, it is well worth understanding it! It is helpful to us that His disciples questioned Him about its meaning (as described in the parallel account in Luke 8:9), and He gave its interpretation in Matthew 13:18–23.

In the parable, the same good seed was sown by the same sower on four different kinds of soil. Therefore, the different results in the four cases were due only to initial differences in the soil. The effects of those conditions were inevitably worked out over time.

In verse 19 (corresponding with Luke 8:11–12), we are told that the seed which was sown represents the word of God being preached, and the soil represents the hearts of those hearing the word. The seed the sower had sown (the word that was preached) in Matthew 13:5, 20 on the *stony* places (hearts) was **received with joy**, and immediately they sprang up. To the human observer, they looked healthy and vigorous. However, when the sun rose in verses 6 and 21, they withered away *because* they had no root.

It is essential to understanding the parable to observe that the sun's rising did not cause them to **lose** their root so that they withered away. Rather, it **exposed** the hidden condition, which had existed all along, that they had no root.

None of the apostles (despite being holy men, in a very close fellowship, under perfect teaching, and Judas Iscariot being one of

---

[91] That is shown from the parallel passage in Mark 4:13: "*And He said to them, 'Do you not understand this parable? How then will you understand all the parables?'*"

the most evil men who has ever lived[92]) had *any* suspicion Judas was not truly Jesus' disciple.[93] However, he is not an exception. Judas was never truly a disciple who later turned from following Jesus. We are told that he was a devil and would betray Jesus in John 6:70–71. We also learn in John 12:6 that Judas *"was a thief."* He loved money more than Jesus (and his own soul).

We are told in Matthew 7 that many who call Jesus *"Lord, Lord"* will not inherit the kingdom of heaven—including some who have even prophesied in His name, cast out demons in His name, and done *many* wonders in His name (which Judas also did, as Matt. 10:1–4 and Mark 3:14–15 show). Instead, Jesus will command them to depart from Him: *"Not everyone who says to Me, 'Lord, Lord,' shall enter the kingdom of heaven ... Many will say to Me in that day, 'Lord, Lord, have we not prophesied in Your name, cast out demons in Your name, and done many wonders [miracles] in Your name?' And then I will declare to them, 'I never knew you; depart from Me, you who practice lawlessness!'"* (vv. 21–23) But we are shown in that passage that none of those were *ever* truly Jesus' disciples, because He will declare to them all, *"I never knew you."*

Nor does 2 Peter 2:20–22 describe true disciples who later turned from following Jesus. In that passage, we read of some who *"through the knowledge of the Lord and Savior Jesus Christ"* escape the defilements of the world, and experience a degree of sanctification, only to be entangled again and overcome by those sins. We are told about them that **after knowing** the way of righteousness, they *turned* from the holy commandment delivered to them, and their last state was worse than their first (though at the first they were unbelievers). Finally, we are taught that what happened to them is according to the proverb that a washed sow *turns* to wallowing in the mud.

---

[92] For, in John 17:12, Jesus called Judas *"the son of perdition,"* using the same four Greek words and inflections used to describe the Antichrist in 2 Thess. 2:3.
[93] Even on the night in which he was going to betray Jesus, and even after Jesus had said one of them would betray him.

Note that those who turned from following Jesus are described as only sows that were washed (as Jesus also washed Judas' feet in John 13:10–11). They were never saved and made new creations— Jesus' sheep. And Jesus is not a shepherd of washed sows. They are similar to those who had at one time **received** the word of God with joy and had what looked to the human observer like good and healthy responses to it, yet had no root.

Earlier in that chapter, 2 Peter 2:14–17 describes those "*carousing in their own deceptions while they feast with you, having ... **forsaken the right way** and gone astray, following the way of **Balaam** ... for whom is reserved the blackness of darkness forever*." Incredibly, the prophet Balaam—with open eyes—described his own unrighteousness and sad estate in Numbers 24:3, 16: "*The utterance of the man whose eyes are opened ... The utterance of him who **hears the words of God**, and has the **knowledge of the Most High**, who sees the vision of the Almighty, who **falls down**, with eyes wide open.*"

Hebrews 3:12–14 teaches that those who fall away from God were never saved by Christ (to become partakers of Christ). Therefore, it warns us to be careful about the condition of our heart: "*Take care, brethren [you who have fellowship with us—having a present profession and appearance of following Christ], that there not be in any one of you an evil [unrepentant], unbelieving heart that falls away from the living God. ... For we **have become** partakers of Christ, **if we hold fast** the beginning of our assurance firm **until the end***" (NASB; see also Heb. 3:6). Similar to John 8:31, this passage teaches that our holding "*firm until the end*" exposes what "*we **have become**.*"

Perhaps 1 John 2:19 contains the plainest teaching that all those who have been saved will, in actuality, continue in repentance. It says of some who turned from following Jesus, "*They went out from us, but they were not really of us*" (NASB). Then it tells us by what reason we are *shown* "*they were not really of us*" (that they were *never* true Christians during the time they were "*with us*," even though we may have thought they were): "***For if they had been** of us, they would have **continued** with us.*" This reason has nothing to do with who they are or any of the particular details of their turning away. Instead, the reason applies to any who at some time appear to be Christians: Those who are truly of us will continue with us.

7.6 Backsliding

The Scriptures show that it is possible for true Christians to slip back into a pattern of willfully sinning, unrepentantly, for a period of time.[94] Some call that behavior "backsliding." If that occurs, those who are spiritual in the church should try to restore them (Gal. 6:1). But if they continue overtaken in that sin, then they must be put out of the church (as 1 Cor. 5 describes). The hope is that this church discipline will be a means of renewing them to repentance (or perhaps bringing them to true repentance for the first time). Thankfully, 2 Corinthians 2 appears to show that the one who was put out of the church according to 1 Corinthians 5, did end up coming to repentance as a result.

Note that the abnormal behavior called backsliding is different from the normal process of sanctification. Chapter 9 more fully describes the relationship between repentance and sanctification.

---

[94] See, for example, Gal. 6:1 and 1 Cor. 5:1, 5.

Chapter 8

What About John's Gospel?

But these are written that you may believe that
Jesus is the Christ, the Son of God.
—John 20:31

The Greek words for *repent* (*metanoeo*) and *repentance* (*metanoia*) appear fifty-eight times in the New Testament. Although John penned the word *metanoeo* in twelve of the thirty-four places that word appears, it is interesting to observe that neither of those specific words appears in his Gospel. Both of those words appear in each of the three other Gospels—Matthew, Mark, and Luke.

On the other hand, the Greek word for *grace* (Strong's #5485, transliterated here *charis*) appears more than 150 times in the New Testament, and John penned only six of them. It is interesting to observe that the word *grace/charis* does not appear in either of the first two Gospels—Matthew and Mark. The first time *grace* appears in the New Testament is in Luke's Gospel, where it is used eight times. In John's Gospel, after appearing three times in the span of four verses in the first chapter, *grace* does not appear again in the rest of that book! The remaining three times it appears in John's other books are simply in blessings and greetings (for instance, in Rev. 1:4, "*Grace to you and peace*").

Some who observe that the words *repent* and *repentance* do not appear in John's Gospel claim that the message of repentance is also missing. Therefore, they argue, it cannot be necessary to repent to be saved. For example, Zane Hodges wrote in his book *Absolutely*

Free!:[95]

> The fourth evangelist explicitly claims to be doing evange-
> lism (John 20:30-31). … Clearly, the message of John's
> Gospel is complete and adequate without any reference to
> repentance whatsoever. … The fourth gospel says nothing
> at all about repentance, much less does it connect
> repentance in any way with eternal life. … Only a resolute
> blindness can resist the obvious conclusion: *John did not
> regard repentance as a condition for eternal life.* If he had,
> he would have said so. After all, that's what his book is all
> about: obtaining eternal life (John 20:30-31). [Italics his.]

Regarding this specific argument by itself, it can be settled in one
sentence: Even if it were true that John's Gospel is silent on
repentance (which it is not, as we have seen), a book's *silence* on a
doctrine that is established by a number of verses in other books does
not refute or invalidate those verses' teaching. Any argument that is
based on such reasoning can be rejected out of hand, for "*the entirety
of Your word is truth*" (Ps. 119:160). If the *whole Bible* were silent
on repentance as a condition for eternal life, we could argue against
the necessity of repentance based on *that* silence.

Nevertheless, carefully examining Hodges' argument that attempts to
make that case is helpful to refine an understanding of some concepts, and expound on principles, that should be generally applied

---

[95] Zane Hodges, *Absolutely Free! A Biblical Reply to Lordship Salvation*,
2nd ed. (Corinth, TX: Grace Evangelical Society, 2014, ISBN 978-
0988347205), 130–131. Hodges taught at Dallas Theological Seminary for
27 years, and for a time served as Chairman of the New Testament
Department. In the first paragraph of the Foreword to *Absolutely Free!*,
Robert Wilkin described a board meeting of the Grace Evangelical Society
in 1989 in which they spoke about *Absolutely Free!* just prior to its first
edition being printed. He wrote, "Several of the board members argued
strongly that Zane should pull the chapter on repentance … They reasoned
that **no one would buy a book** dealing with clarity in evangelism that
argued that **repentance is not a condition of everlasting life** [emphasis
added]." But Hodges insisted on keeping that chapter (from which the quote
is taken)—and how different things are now.

when trying to understand what God has written to us in the Bible. Therefore, appendix A does that in significant detail. However, that lengthy treatment should not be misunderstood as dignifying the argument itself.

But why would God, in His wisdom, avoid using the words *repent* and *repentance* in John's Gospel? It does not appear that the Scriptures provide an answer to that question in a manner that can be proved. But in thinking of a possibility, a promising place to start might be John 20:30-31, since it tells us why some things were omitted from that Gospel, while others were included: "*Truly Jesus did many other signs ... which are **not written** in this book; but **these** are written that you may believe that Jesus is the Christ, the Son of God.*"

This passage tells us that the things specially selected to be written in the book of John are those that help persuade someone to believe in Jesus. Section 3.1 described the relationship and ordering of faith and repentance: It is those who believe in Jesus who *then* repent, and not those who repent who then believe in Jesus. Perhaps that relationship underlies the absence of the words *repent* and *repentance* in John's Gospel—whose special purpose is to help people believe in Jesus.

Although those specific words do not appear, the need to repent to have eternal life is evident in John. So too, God's grace can be seen in Matthew and Mark, though the word *grace* cannot.

The line of reasoning behind the suggested answer might be tested (though certainly not proved) by seeing if it can be used to explain the absence of the word *grace* in both Matthew and Mark. The answer is yes, that line of reasoning can explain that absence as well.

Section 3.3 described the special emphasis of each of the four Gospels. The emphasis in Matthew, to convince us of our sins and condemnation, is, by itself, independent of grace. Perhaps less apparent, Mark's emphasis that Jesus is **able** to forgive our sins and deliver us from any peril does not, alone, show His grace toward us personally. It is only when that ability underpins the emphasis in

Luke—if you come to Jesus in repentance, He **will** forgive and save you—that grace is shown.

Chapter 9

Repentance and Sanctification

I thought about my ways, and turned my feet to Your testimonies.
—Psalm 119:59

In 1 Peter 1:15, Christians are commanded, *"According to the Holy One who has called you, you also become holy in all conduct"* (LITV). Those who are saved become progressively more holy in their conduct. Over time, they sin less and grow in sanctification. Second Peter 1:5–7 charges us, *"Giving all diligence, add to your faith virtue, to virtue knowledge, to knowledge self-control, to self-control perseverance, to perseverance godliness, to godliness brotherly kindness, and to brotherly kindness love."* And Romans 12:2 entreats, *"Do not be conformed to this world, but be transformed by the renewing of your mind, that you may prove what is that good and acceptable and perfect will of God."*

When Paul wrote to the Corinthian church, he made clear that more sanctified behavior is expected of mature Christians than infants in Christ. But he described how some in Corinth were still behaving as infants in Christ. He said that he *"could not speak to you as to [mature]* **spiritual men,**[96] *but [he had to speak to them] as to men of*

---

[96] Here, the Greek adjective meaning *spiritual* is used as a noun (as a substantive adjective) that is rendered *"spiritual men."* In using this adjective as a noun to refer to this group (similar to using the adjective meek as a noun in the phrase "the meek"), it describes them as **characterized** by being spiritual. It refers to those who have progressed significantly in their sanctification and spirituality. This verse contrasts that group with *"infants in Christ."*

*flesh [some translations render this carnal], as to **infants in Christ***" (1 Cor. 3:1 NASB).

Paul described the *manner* in which the Christians in Corinth were behaving as infants in Christ in verse 3: "*For since there is **jealousy** and **strife** among you, are you not fleshly, and are you not walking like mere men?*" (NASB) According to these verses, we would not expect jealousy and strife among mature Christians, though it is normal for the unsaved ("*men of flesh*"/"*mere men*"), and is also expected of "*infants in Christ.*"

However, do not think that progressive sanctification is the result of progressive repentance. As has been well proved, Jesus does not accept those who come to Him without desiring to obey Him. In essence, such people are saying to Him, "Look, I'll do these things You've commanded, but not those, though I might change my mind later." And then, as time goes on, they might tell Him, "Well, okay, I'll do two of those things also, but still not these others."

Put another way, you must come to Jesus with your whole heart— not with a divided heart that may become somewhat less divided over time. There are no degrees in the repentance which is to life: A person is either repentant or unrepentant.

If those who are saved are truly repentant, and have resolved to follow Jesus in all things, why are they not holy in all their conduct from the moment of their salvation? Why is sanctification a process?

One obvious reason is that when someone is saved, they do not have, and are not given, a perfect knowledge of God's commands and His will in all situations. In fact, the Greek word that is translated *disciple* means "a learner."[97] Seeking to know God's will is a distinguishing characteristic of the repentant.

Conversely, a characteristic of the wicked is that they do not seek to know God's will, and that is a reason given in Psalm 119:155 that they do not find salvation: "*Salvation is far from the wicked, for they*

---

[97] Strong, *Dictionary of the Greek Testament*, 45, #3101.

do not seek Your statutes." By contrast, the writer of Psalm 119 prayed in many places for God to give him an understanding of His commands. For instance, in verse 33 he said, "*Teach me the way of Your Statutes, and I will keep it to the end*" (LITV).

The primary means of learning God's will is through God's Word, the Bible. Therefore, when Jesus prayed for the sanctification of His disciples in John 17:17, He said, "*Sanctify them **by** Your truth. **Your word** is truth.*" Accordingly, the psalmist answered his rhetorical question in Psalm 119:9, "*How can a young man cleanse his way?*" saying, "*By taking heed according to Your word. ... Your word I have hidden in my heart, that I might not sin against You*" (vv. 9, 11). And in verse 105, he described how God's Word shows him the way in which he should walk, saying, "*Your word is a lamp to my feet and a light to my path.*"

Another reason sanctification is a process is that all Christians stumble. Although they may know the way in which they should walk in a particular matter, and have set their hearts to do so, they can still stumble in that matter for various reasons (such as being seduced by lusts, fear, etc.). Peter had resolved that even if he had to die with Jesus, he would not deny Him. Although he did deny Jesus that very night, later he was faithful in his testimony even until death (glorifying God by that death, as John 21:19 tells us).

Those who do not want to stumble learn over time how to walk so as to overcome the causes of their stumbling. For some particular sins, that may include not looking at or doing things, at least for a while, which may tempt them to sin.

In a surprising warning in Matthew 5:30, Jesus taught us how serious our sins (stumblings) are and, therefore, how earnest we should be in cleansing ourselves from them. He said, "*If your right hand makes you stumble, cut it off and throw it from you; for it is better for you to lose one of the parts of your body, than for your whole body to go into hell*" (NASB). He gave similar teaching in Matthew 5:29 and 18:8–9.

As a separate issue, some may think this specific example is so extreme that Jesus did not intend for it to be taken as truth, but as hyperbole. If one thinks that Jesus' instruction here is hyperbole, then other teachings of His are also suspect. And in those cases, one is left to imagine what is truly enjoined.

Happily, however, that is not the case. Jesus not only taught a principle here in an indelible way, but His surprising, specific example, which rouses us to examine our walk and faith, is also literally true: If our right hand makes us stumble, we should cut it off and throw it from us. Through this specific example, He confronts both unbelief and wrong ideas about our sins in those who stumble at this teaching.

When people are told by their physician they will soon die if their right hand (which has gangrene, or cancer, etc.) is not amputated, we naturally expect that (if they believe and trust their physician) they will have it amputated. People generally prefer losing "one of the parts of their body" than to lose their life.[98] Then how much more should we expect people would even cut off their right hand if the Great Physician were to tell them it is required to escape the fire of hell and have eternal life? Whether or not they take such drastic action is simply a matter of whether they believe and trust the Great Physician.

In His teaching, Jesus commanded what you should do in the specific, hypothetical case that "*your right hand makes you stumble.*" However, it is not out of one's right hand that thefts proceed, but "*out of the **heart** come evil thoughts, murders, adulteries, fornications, thefts, false witness, slanders*" (Matt. 15:19 NASB). A man who, like Judas, is stumbling in the sin of stealing should know it is his heart that motivates him to steal with his right hand, not his hand acting independently of his heart's desires and purposes.

Consider a hypothetical, deluded man who does not realize that is the case and, being zealous to believe and follow Christ, amputates his right hand. He would soon discover that his "*heart being busied with*

---

[98] I am indebted to a Bible commentary that made this observation about what people with dire physical ailments are willing to do for their lives in this world, but I cannot locate it at this time.

covetousness" (2 Pet. 2:14 LITV) is motivating him to steal with his left hand! And Jesus did not teach in His hypothetical example that we should cut off "all parts of our body" that make us stumble. He did not say, for instance, "If your hands make you stumble, cut them both off." Nor did He say to cut out your heart.

Through it all, our zealous but deluded man should realize that it was not his right hand that he needed to throw from him, but he needed to cast away from himself his transgressions, repenting from stealing and the covetousness in his heart, and get a new heart. God instructs us in Ezekiel 18:30–32: "*'Repent, and ... Cast away from you all the transgressions which you have committed, and get yourselves a new heart ... For I have no pleasure in the death of one who dies,' says the Lord GOD. 'Therefore turn and live!'*"

When people who have repented and continue in repentance learn that they have been unknowingly walking in a sin, they repent from that particular sin. That is, they purpose not to sin in that way ever again. Or, if they have stumbled and sinned in something they knew to be sin and had resolved not to sin in it, they repent from that sin again—renewing their resolve to walk in such a way so as to keep themselves from stumbling in it again, and asking God to give them grace to do so (Heb. 4:15–16).

These are some of the ways by which Christians progress in sanctification. This is part of what the command in Philippians 2:12 means: "*Work out your salvation with fear and trembling*" (NASB).

Chapter 10

Repentance Summary

Whoever loses his life for My sake, he is the one who will save it.
—Luke 9:24 NASB

The Bible teaches us that repentance is foundational to the gospel and salvation. In Luke 5:32, Jesus told us that He *came* to call sinners to repentance. In the list in Hebrews 6:1–2 of those things which are said to be the first principles of the oracles of God, repentance is listed first. It is listed there ahead of faith, the resurrection of the dead, and eternal judgment. Repentance is a requirement of the first and great commandment in the Law. It is not surprising that both the first word of preaching in the New Testament and the first word of Jesus' recorded preaching is *"Repent."*

Repentance for the forgiveness of sins should be preached in Jesus' name, and we see that borne out in the apostles' preaching. The person who "believes" in Jesus, yet is unrepentant, will not be saved, but is like the demons who cried out about Jesus, *"You are the Christ, the Son of God!"* (Luke 4:41) Jesus will not forgive the sins of those who *intend* to *continue* in their sins.

Although you must acknowledge your sins in order to repent from them, and you ought to feel grief and remorse over them, repentance is not how you feel about something you have done. It is not regret looking back, but your purposes going forward. Repentance is not a work, but a resolve. To repent is to *turn* from walking in any and all of your sins and to *resolve* to follow Jesus. True faith and true repentance, although they are different things, always come together

115

(repentance following faith). Though striving to do God's will is not repentance, it is a sure fruit of repentance. Unlike sanctification, true repentance is not progressive. A person is either repentant or unrepentant.

Psalm 119:4 says of God, "*You have commanded us to keep Your precepts diligently.*" The psalmist summarized his repentant response in verse 106, "*I have sworn and confirmed that I will keep Your righteous judgments.*" If you find that you have stumbled off, or wandered from, or did not know, the way in which you should walk, then repent and get (back) on it. As the psalmist said in verse 59, "*I thought about my ways, and turned my feet to Your testimonies.*"

People must repent from their sins for Jesus to forgive and save them, and must continue in repentance to inherit eternal life. Nevertheless, the Good Shepherd will not lose any of His sheep. In Luke 9:23–25, Jesus said to all (both the crowd and His disciples, as Mark 8:34 shows), "*If anyone wishes to come after Me, he must deny himself, and take up his cross daily and follow Me. For whoever wishes to save his life will lose it, but whoever loses his life for My sake, he is the one who will save it. For what is a man profited if he gains the whole world, and loses or forfeits himself?*" (NASB) Those who would come to Jesus must come with no conditions, understanding that a man is profited nothing in gaining the whole world yet losing himself.

To repent is to resolve, "Jesus, whatever may come, I will follow You."

If you realize that you have not continued in repentance, it does not matter whether you have ever truly repented. If, believing in Jesus, you want to follow Him, then repent, and continue in repentance, and bear fruits in keeping with repentance.

Chapter 11

What About Grace?

Do not set aside the grace of God.
—Galatians 2:21

Someone may ask, "It is because of grace that God forgives our sins and saves us. If I have to repent from my sins to be saved, then where is grace?"

This question is based on an impression that if repentance is thought to be necessary, then God's grace in salvation is diminished or even rejected. Likewise, a very similar question could be added to it, "And if I have to believe in Jesus to be saved, then where is grace?" How important these questions are, since we have surely seen that the Bible teaches faith and repentance are necessary for God to save someone!

Before looking at the harmony between repentance and grace that we know must exist, it is interesting to observe their harmony asserted right from the beginning of the New Testament. John the Baptist, who began the New Testament's preaching with the command to repent, was given his name by God (Luke 1:13). And we are told that his name was unexpected—for *"there is no one among ... [his] relatives who is called by this name"* (v. 61). But what a beautiful name it is. The Greek name rendered *John* is often translated "The LORD Has Been Gracious."[99] Then, this one who came preaching

---

[99] The Greek name rendered "John" is Strong's #2491 and is from the Hebrew name that is Strong's #3110, which in turn is a shortened form of

"repentance for the forgiveness of sins" (Mark 1:4 NASB) has a name that declares God's grace![100]

11.1 The Gift of God

Romans 6:23 states, *"The wages of sin is death, but the gift of God is eternal life in Christ Jesus our Lord."* It is only by God's grace that people's sins can be forgiven and they can be saved. No one is deserving of that gift, and there is nothing a sinful person can do to earn, achieve, or merit it. As Romans 3:23–24 tells us, *"For all have sinned and fall short of the glory of God, being justified as a gift by His grace through the redemption which is in Christ Jesus"* (NASB).

However, as has been thoroughly shown by many passages in previous chapters, God only saves by His grace those who call on Him to save them, believing in Jesus and repenting from their sins. A few of those passages are Romans 10:13–14, Acts 16:31, John 8:24, Luke 13:5, and Acts 2:38. An expression of that truth from the mid-1600's in The Westminster Confession of Faith was quoted in a footnote in chapter 3: "Although repentance be not … any satisfaction for sin, … none may expect pardon without it."

But there is no conflict (as there cannot be) between the truths expressed in the preceding two paragraphs. Their compatibility can be easily understood when one is careful not to confuse the following four separate issues, which are expressed as questions below. After each question, a parenthetical answer is given and shown by references that are taken from the preceding two paragraphs:

1. What are **the means** by which someone is forgiven and saved?
   (God grants forgiveness of sins and saves a person by His grace—*"a gift by His grace."*)

---

the Hebrew name that is Strong's #3076. The translation of the name shown here is a common translation of that Hebrew name, and can be found, for example, in *NAS Exhaustive Concordance of the Bible with Hebrew-Aramaic and Greek Dictionaries* (1998). Retrieved August 13, 2022, from https://biblehub.com/nasec/hebrew/3076.htm

[100] Special thanks to my son John for this observation.

2. What was **required for God to be able to** forgive our
   sins and save us?
   (The Son of God needed to take up our sins in His body
   and be crucified as a sacrifice for those sins—*"through
   the redemption which is in Christ Jesus."*)
3. What does **God require in order to** forgive and save a
   sinner?
   (A sinner must call on the name of the Lord to be saved
   with faith and repentance—Rom. 10:13–14, Acts 16:31,
   John 8:24, Luke 13:5, and Acts 2:38.)
4. Do **any deserve** to have their sins forgiven and be saved?
   (Absolutely not—*"all have sinned and fall short"* and
   "the wages of sin is death.")

11.2 We Must Not Despise God's Grace

What is more, the reality is **exactly the opposite** of the impression
behind the question at the beginning of this chapter. God's grace
gives us more reason to be repentant. A passage in Hebrews 10:26–
30 shows this. Recall that its first two verses were discussed in some
detail in section 7.2:

> *For if we go on sinning **willfully** after receiving the
> knowledge of the truth, there no longer remains a sacrifice
> for sins, but a terrifying expectation of judgment and the
> fury of a fire which will consume the adversaries. Anyone
> who has set aside the Law of Moses dies without mercy on
> the testimony of two or three witnesses. How much severer
> punishment do you think he will deserve who has trampled
> under foot the Son of God, and has regarded as unclean
> the blood of the covenant by which he was sanctified, and
> **has insulted the Spirit of grace**? For we know Him who
> said, "Vengeance is Mine, I will repay." And again, "The
> LORD will judge His people."* (NASB)

Those who *"go on sinning **willfully**"* are unrepentant. And this
passage tells us that those who do so *"after receiving the knowledge
of the truth"* have *"trampled under foot the Son of God"* and
"insulted the Spirit of grace." God's great grace toward us, at the
cost of the sacrifice of His Son, is given in this passage as a reason

those who have received the knowledge of the truth must not go on sinning willfully. For to do so is to despise that grace—it is to trample under foot God's Son and insult God's Spirit of grace! Therefore, those who do so bring "*a terrifying expectation of judgment and the fury of a fire*" upon themselves.

Matthew Henry's Commentary, expounding on Hebrews 10:26–30, says, "How dreadful is the case when not only the *justice* of God, but his *abused grace and mercy* call for vengeance!"[101] (Emphasis added.)

Paradoxically then, the question at the beginning of this chapter could be prompted by a way of thinking that *despises "the grace of God [which] has appeared [to us now under the New Covenant], bringing salvation to all men"* (Titus 2:11 NASB).

A passage in Luke 23:33–43 describes two men who witnessed that grace in the same extraordinary way, but had two very different reactions. They were the two criminals who were crucified with Jesus. As they witnessed the Son of God on the cross, the wonder of God's great grace was worked out in front of them as never before or since. And in verse 34, they heard Jesus pray for those putting Him to death, "*Father, forgive them, for they do not know what they do.*"

One of the criminals despised that grace, and his contempt for it became a stumbling block which kept him from believing in Jesus. In verse 39, we read that he blasphemed Jesus, saying, "*If You are the Christ, save Yourself and us.*" Two of the thoughts behind his exclamation could be expressed, "If You were the Christ, You would be able to save Yourself, and You would surely also save us."

Although the circumstances are different, there is a similarity between what he expressed and what people frequently express when a calamity occurs: "If there is a good God in heaven, then why did *this* happen??" His exclamation demonstrated two misunderstandings which are common for people to have and, indeed, go hand in hand.

---

[101] *Matthew Henry's Commentary on the Whole Bible*, 2397.

First, he did not understand how just and well-deserved his punishment was. As a result, he thought that if Jesus was the Christ, He would save him from this injustice. Second, he did not understand why it was necessary for the Christ to be crucified. He thought that if Jesus was the Christ, He would save Himself. Of course, as we saw in section 7.2, Jesus was *able* to save Himself. He told us in Matthew 26:53, "*Do you think that I am not able now to call on My Father, and He will place beside Me more than twelve legions of angels?*" (LITV) But if the Good Shepherd was to save the sheep, He could not save Himself. He needed to lay down His life for the sheep (John 10:11, 15).

To sum it up, this condemned criminal had no need of a Messiah who would die for his sins. The same was true of those at the other end of the religious social scale—the chief priests and elders and scribes—who said in Matthew 27:42, mocking, "*If He is the King of Israel, let Him now come down from the cross, and we will believe Him.*" They needed a Messiah who would lead them to victory over their oppressors and give them the position they deserved in the world. Because they did not understand what they deserved, they understood neither the need for God's grace nor its *great cost*. There is a hymn which well says:

> Ye who think of sin but lightly
> Nor suppose the evil great
> Here may view its nature rightly,
> Here its guilt may estimate.
> Mark the Sacrifice appointed,
> See who bears the awful load.[102]

However, the other criminal that was crucified with Jesus rebuked the first criminal—knowing that their punishment was deserved, but that Jesus had done nothing wrong: "*But the other answered, and rebuking him said, 'Do you not even fear God, since you are under the same sentence of condemnation? And we indeed are suffer-*

---

[102] Thomas Kelly, "Stricken, Smitten, and Afflicted," 1804. Reprinted in *Trinity Hymnal*, hymn 192. Note that the name of the hymn was inspired by Isa. 53:4.

ing justly, for we are receiving what we deserve for our deeds; but this man has done nothing wrong" (Luke 23:40–41 NASB).

This crucified criminal gave the only recorded rebuke to those who were mocking and blaspheming the Christ on the cross. Through the events unfolding before his eyes, he came to know that "*this man*" Jesus is the Christ. He knew that Jesus had never sinned, and confessed himself to be a justly condemned sinner. He also knew that after Jesus' death, "*the King of Israel*" would rule in His eternal kingdom. And so he begged Jesus, saying, "***Lord**, remember me when You come into Your kingdom*" (v. 42). Whereupon, "*Jesus said to him, 'Assuredly, I say to you, today you will be with Me in Paradise*'" (v. 43).

How great a salvation we are now offered through "*the gospel of the grace of God*" (Acts 20:24)! The Law has been called "*the ministry of death*" and "*the ministry of condemnation*" (2 Cor. 3:7, 9), whereas the ministry of the New Covenant has been called "*the ministry of reconciliation*" (2 Cor. 5:18).

In Hebrews 2:1–3, we are warned that having so great a salvation now provided to us by God's grace requires us to pay much closer attention to what God has spoken to us under the New Covenant: "*For **this reason** we must pay **much closer attention** to what we have heard ... For if ... [**under the Law**] every transgression and disobedience received a just penalty, how will **we escape** if we neglect **so great a salvation?**"* (NASB) The answer to this rhetorical question is that those who are neglectful of it have no hope of escape.

Chapter 12

Amazing Grace

The law was given through Moses,
but grace and truth came through Jesus Christ.
—John 1:17

Few things are as important to Christianity as grace. Without grace, the Word of God would not have become flesh and dwelt among us. Without grace, the sinless Son of God would not have taken up our sins in His body to the cross, offering Himself a sacrifice for our sins and dying for us. Without grace, our sins could not be forgiven, and there would be no gospel to preach. Without grace, God would not show kindness to those living in rebellion against Him, giving them time to repent. Without grace, the repentant would not be able to walk in His ways and do the works He has given them to do. Without grace, we would not be able to love our enemies. And without grace, death would not be swallowed up in victory.

In describing the excellencies of our Lord Jesus, John 1:17 compares what came through Jesus Christ to that which was given through Moses: "*The law was given through Moses, but grace and truth came through Jesus Christ.*"

It is written of the Messiah in Psalm 45:2, "*You are fairer than the sons of men; grace is poured upon Your lips.*" The reason expressed there that He is fairer than the sons of men is that grace is poured upon His lips. Consistently, the Scriptures do not say that grace is poured upon the lips of any other man. John testified of this glorious attribute of Jesus in John 1:14: "*And we beheld His glory, the glory as of the only begotten of the Father, full of grace and truth.*"

12.1 God's Greatest Grace
Surely the greatest demonstration of God's amazing grace is Jesus' offering of Himself a sacrifice for our sins on the cross— "*the One having given Himself a ransom on behalf of all, the testimony to be given in its own time, to which I [Paul] was appointed a herald and apostle*" (1 Tim. 2:6–7 LITV). As John 3:16 says, in describing how great God's love for the world is, "*For God so loved the world that He gave His only begotten Son.*"

It is clear, as Jesus stated in John 15:13, that a man has no greater love for his friends than to lay down his life for them. But on the cross, Jesus demonstrated that greatest love for His enemies! Romans 5:8 and 10 tell us, "*God demonstrates His own love toward us, in that while we were **still sinners**, Christ died for us ... **when we were enemies.**"*

What Jesus did when He died for us on the cross is described in 1 Peter 2:21–24: "*Christ also suffered for our sake, ... who did no sin, nor was deceit found in His mouth; ... who Himself took up our sins in His body to the tree, in order that we, after dying to sins, might live to righteousness; of whom by His bruise you were healed*" (ATR).

12.2 Our Greatest Need for Grace
But what difference would it make to us if Jesus had not died for our sins? It is the difference between certain eternal punishment and the hope of eternal blessing. A passage beginning in Romans 3:19 tells us that "*all the world*" is "*guilty before God*" because, as verse 23 summarizes, "*all have sinned.*" Romans 2:5 begins one of many passages that tell us a day of judgment is coming: "*The day of wrath and revelation of the righteous judgment of God*" (NASB). The only possibility for us to escape God's judgment is for God to forgive our sins and to justify us—"counting" righteousness to us.[103]

---

[103] See Rom. 3:23–24. The first eight verses of Rom 4. describe how God did those things for Abraham (before the Law) and David (under the Law).

Some may wonder how it is that sin could come with both so great a penalty and one we are powerless to escape by our will or actions. Yet we are all familiar with similar situations. There are so many things in this life which, if done, will drastically change the rest of our lives (and others)—if not end those lives altogether—no matter what we may later wish or do.

For example, if you lose your balance at the edge of a cliff, you will be judged by the law of gravity—no matter how much you regret your carelessness as you are falling, and resolve never to be so careless again. No matter how you might beg the law of gravity to show mercy, it will inexorably act without partiality according to its precepts. As another example, you might become distracted for a moment when driving a vehicle with your family in it. Or, you might eat something that is poisonous.

We are given the terrible example of Adam, the first man, in the first few pages of our Bible. That incident with Adam also explains why the creation we see around us is no longer "*very good*" (Gen. 1:31).

Adam was abundantly provided for, and there was nothing withheld from him except one thing: He could freely eat of every tree in the garden except one. And the reason he was forbidden to eat of that one was because if he did, he would surely die (Gen. 2:16–17)! After he disobeyed God and ate of that tree, "*sin entered the world ... and death through sin, so also death passed to **all** men*" (Rom. 5:12 LITV).

Romans 5:18–19 further describes the consequences of Adam's transgression to all of his descendants, saying, "*Through one trans-gression there resulted condemnation to all men ... For ... through the one man's disobedience the many [all of Adam's descendants] were made sinners*" (NASB).

In it, Rom. 4:6–8 says, "*Even as also David says of the blessedness of the man to whom God counts righteousness apart from works: 'Blessed are those whose lawlessnesses are forgiven, and whose sins are covered; blessed the man to whom the Lord will in no way charge sin'*" (LITV).

However, no matter what may befall us, or that we might bring upon ourselves in this life, we have a merciful and almighty God who stands ready to redeem all who turn to Him. And any afflictions we might endure in this life, which can only be momentary, are described as a light thing compared with the weighty and eternal blessings which God has laid up in heaven for those who are Jesus' sheep: "*For our light affliction, which is but for a moment, is working for us a far more exceeding and eternal weight of glory*" (2 Cor. 4:17).

Indeed, we are told that *no one* has even *imagined* how amazing and wonderful those blessings will be: "*Eye has not seen, nor ear heard, nor have entered into the heart of man the things which God has prepared for those who love Him*" (1 Cor. 2:9). And with those blessings in the new heaven and new earth (Rev. 21:1), we are told there will be "*no ... pain*" "*nor sorrow*" (Rev. 21:4).

God would like everyone to have those blessings—as it is written about Him in Ezekiel 33:11: "*'As I live,' says the Lord GOD, 'I have no pleasure in the death of the wicked, but that the wicked turn from his way and live. Turn, turn from your evil ways! For why should you die?'*" The same is expressed in 2 Peter 3:9: "*The Lord is ... not willing that any should perish but that all should come to repentance.*"

People are kept from those blessings only by their unwillingness to believe in Him and repent from their sins. As Jesus said to some who did not believe in Him in John 5:40, "*You are unwilling to come to Me so that you may have life*" (NASB).

Two entire chapters—from Matthew 24:3 through the end of Matthew 25—are devoted to Jesus' teaching about His return at the end of the age to take account with us. In that passage, in Matthew 25:31–46, He began a description of the day of judgment by saying, "*When the Son of Man comes in His glory, and all the holy angels with Him, then He will sit on the throne of His glory. All the nations will be gathered before Him*" (vv. 31–32).

He said that He will then separate those gathered before Him "*as a shepherd divides his sheep from the goats. And He will set the sheep on His right hand, but the goats on the left. Then the King will say to those on His right hand, 'Come, you blessed of My Father, inherit the kingdom prepared for you'"* (vv. 32–34). In verse 41, Jesus told us that He will say to all those who are not His sheep, *"Depart from Me, accursed ones, into **the eternal fire** which has been **prepared for the devil** and his angels"* (NASB). And in verse 46, Jesus said, *"These will go away into **eternal punishment**, but the righteous into eternal life"* (NASB).

The eternal fire mentioned in verse 41, which will torment the devil, his angels, and all who are not Jesus' sheep, is called *"the lake of fire [and brimstone]."* Revelation 20:10 shows this: *"And the devil who deceived them was thrown into **the lake of fire and brimstone**, where the beast and the false prophet are also; and they will be **tormented** day and night **forever and ever**"* (NASB). Like Matthew 25:41, Revelation 20:15 tells us that punishment will also be inflicted on all those who are not Jesus' sheep—whose names are not written in the book of life: *"And if **anyone's** name was not found written in the book of **life**, he was thrown into **the lake of fire**"* (NASB).

Their punishment in the lake of fire will be eternal because that fire will torment without consuming. Instead, as Jesus explained three times in Mark 9, the lake of fire is a place *"where their worm does not die, and the fire is not quenched"* (vv. 44, 46, 48 NASB). *"Their worm"* is a term for the inglorious resurrected bodies of the unrepentant.[104] Although their worm will never die, this punishment in the lake of fire is called the second death. As Revelation 21:8 describes, *"But for the cowardly and unbelieving ... and all liars, their part will be in the lake that burns with fire and brimstone, which is the second death"* (NASB).

12.3 God's Provision for That Grace

If Jesus had not died for our sins, we would not be able to be forgiven, and there would be no escaping our deserved, eternal punishment for those sins. But why would Jesus need to offer

---

[104] That the unrepentant will also be raised out of the graves, see, for example, John 5:28–29 and Dan. 12:2.

Himself a sacrifice for our sins in order for God to be able to forgive them?

The Bible makes plain that God loves righteousness and hates evil. He is also righteous in all His ways. And Romans 3:25–26 tells us that in order for God both to forgive someone's sins who has faith in Jesus, and to be righteous, Jesus' death on the cross—His blood—was necessary. For, speaking of Jesus, it says, "*whom God set forth as a propitiation by His blood, through faith [by His blood Jesus is a propitiation for the sins of those who have faith in Him], to demonstrate His righteousness ... that He might be just **and** the justifier **of** the one who has faith in Jesus.*"

This passage tells us that God could not be both just (righteous) and merciful to those who have faith in Jesus by justifying them (forgiving all their sins and counting righteousness to them) apart from Jesus' offering Himself a sacrifice for those sins. It is easy to think of situations in which showing some specific mercy to someone might require setting aside what is righteous and doing something that is unrighteous. But that would be sinful, for "*all unrighteousness is sin*" (1 John 5:17).

Jesus' sacrifice enables God both to be righteous and to justify those who have faith in Jesus. In a manner of speaking, it enables mercy and righteousness to dwell together in a beautiful and harmonious relationship. Through Jesus' death on the cross, God made that amicable relationship between mercy and righteousness possible, as described in Psalm 85:10, "*Mercy and truth have met together; righteousness and peace have kissed.*"

Note that Romans 3:25–26 specifically states that propitiation by Jesus' blood is "*through faith,*" and that Jesus' death was necessary for God to be just while justifying "*the one who has faith in Jesus.*" Since true faith in Jesus and repentance always come together, Jesus' death was necessary for God to be righteous while forgiving those who are believing and repentant. But the strong implication is that Jesus' death does *not* enable God to be righteous while forgiving those who are unbelieving and unrepentant. As one might expect, there is *no* passage in the Bible that speaks of a provision that would enable God to be just while justifying the unrepentant.

On the cross, we see that God's righteousness and justice are so pure, that when Jesus *"took up our sins in His body to the tree"* (1 Pet. 2:24 ATR), God poured out His wrath upon His beloved Son.[105] But on that same cross, we also see God's mercy and love being greater than, and triumphing over, His judgment and wrath against sin. For Ephesians 2:16 tells us that through the cross, Jesus was *"putting to death the enmity"* between us and God, in order that He might reconcile us to Him.

Accordingly, 2 Corinthians 5:19 tells us, *"God was in Christ reconciling the world to Himself, not counting their trespasses against them"* (NASB). And Colossians 2:14 says that *"having wiped out the handwriting of requirements that was against us, which was contrary to us ... He has taken it out of the way, having nailed it to the cross"*! So we see on the cross that *"mercy triumphs over judgment"* (James 2:13).

12.4 God's Abundant Grace
We can also see God's grace toward all, even to *"the ungracious and evil"* (Luke 6:35 YLT), in many common things that happen daily. In Matthew 5:45, Jesus described how God's grace is manifested by the fact that *"He causes His sun to rise on the evil and the good, and sends rain on the righteous and the unrighteous"* (NASB). If the first manifestation of God's grace described in that verse is grasped, it helps us see myriads of other manifestations of His grace. That manifestation is evident only when God's complete sovereignty over all that happens in His creation is understood.

If there is anything that people might be apt to think is certain to happen without any grace from God, it is that the sun will rise tomorrow, and it will shine on both a man and his neighbor alike. But in Jesus' statement, *"He causes His sun to rise,"* He testifies that the sun is God's sun, and that God is the One who makes it rise.

Accordingly, the Scriptures record a time when God kept the sun

---

[105] See, for example, Ps. 88:6–7, 16, Lam. 1:12–14, Ps. 22:1, and 42:7.

from setting for about the period of a day (Josh. 10:12–13). At another time, He made the sun go back in its path (2 Kings 20:8–11). And He darkened the sun for about three hours over all the earth when Jesus was crucified (Luke 23:44).

But Jesus' statement about God's sovereignty over the rising of "*His sun*" extends even further. In that passage, He makes clear that the reason the sun rises on the evil *as well as* the good is because God "*causes*" that to happen. In other words, if it pleased Him, God could make His sun rise only on the good. We see an example of this power when He made darkness so intense in the land of Egypt that the Egyptians were not able to see anything for three days, while all of the Israelites living alongside them in the land of Egypt had light in their dwellings (Ex. 10:21–23).

Certainly then, God's sovereignty extends to **all** things that happen on the earth. As Psalm 135:6 proclaims, "*Whatever the LORD pleases He does, in heaven and in earth, in the seas and in all deep places.*" In Job 36:32, we are told that God commands the lightning to strike. And in Matthew 10:29, Jesus told us that not even one sparrow falls to the ground apart from our Father's will. Acts 17:25 says that God is the One who gives "*to **all** people life and breath and **all things***" (NASB). This fact is behind John the Baptist's statement in John 3:27, "*A man can receive **nothing** unless it has been given to him from heaven.*"

Therefore, it is God who is not only sending rain on the field of the farmer that blesses Him, but causing it to fall on the field of the farmer that curses Him. Consequently, we personally witness God showing grace every day to people who themselves are unkind and unthankful and evil. Yet He gives them good things, and makes them prosper for a time.

There was a 40-year-old attorney, N. Graves Thomas, who often took notorious clients to defend, such as suspects in organized crime and police killings. An article in the Chicago Tribune on May 27, 1987 describes what happened when Thomas was in his new ski boat on Lake Bistineau in Louisiana—undoubtedly enjoying his prosperity.[106] Three other people were in the boat with him at the time of a thunderstorm, while a young woman was in the water preparing to ski. Witnesses said Thomas stood up in the back of the boat, raised his hands, and proclaimed heavenward, "Here I am!" Then a lightning bolt struck him in the head, apparently killing him immediately. It is not often that we hear of cases in which there is such a swift and severe reply.

Ecclesiastes 8:11 tells us, "*Where sentence on an evil work is not executed speedily, on account of this the heart of the sons of men is fully set in them to do evil*" (LITV). If every impudent challenge of God met with swift retribution, it would not be long before people were loathe to taunt Him. As Isaiah 26:9 observes, "*For when Your judgments are in the earth, the inhabitants of the world will learn righteousness.*"

Through God's power and judgments, He is *able* to make His enemies pretend submission to Him, as Psalm 81:15 tells us: "*The haters of the LORD would pretend submission to Him, but their fate would endure forever.*"[107] But God does not desire nor countenance a form of obedience that is outward only. He accepts only true faith and repentance. Jesus told us that "*those who worship Him must worship in spirit and truth*" (John 4:24 NASB). Accordingly, He instructed us, "*First cleanse the inside of the cup and of the dish, that the outside of them may become clean also*" (Matt. 23:26 LITV).

We should not interpret God's grace toward the ungracious and evil as showing that He approves of, or even tolerates, evil. He corrected that wrong impression some might have when He said, "*These things you have done, and I kept silent; you thought that I was altogether like you; but I will rebuke you, and set them in order before your eyes*" (Ps. 50:21). As we saw in section 3.4, Romans 2:4 tells us the purpose of His kindness and forbearance and long-suffering to the unrepentant is to lead them to repentance. Of course, giving people

---

[106] Lightning Answers Call—Fatally (May 27, 1987). *Chicago Tribune*. Retrieved August 13, 2022, from https://www.chicagotribune.com/news/ct-xpm-1987-05-27-8702090133-story.html
[107] See also Ps. 66:3, Job 41:1–3, and 40:11–12.

time to repent also gives them time to continue in unrepentance—working out evil in the world toward others, and even to crucify the Christ!

Thankfully, our God is a God who hates evil. He will not enable people to work out what is evil forever. And, in the end, justice will be done. Though He is kind to those who are evil and unthankful, though He is forbearing, long-suffering, gracious, and merciful, and so loved the world that He gave His Son to die for our sins, He will ultimately judge those who unrepentantly continue in their sinful ways. He will burn up this present, defiled heavens and earth where evil is done, and create a new heavens and earth which are very good (2 Pet. 3:9–13; Rev. 21:1). And *they* will never be defiled (Rev. 21:4–5, 27).

Paul, who had zealously persecuted Christians as an unbeliever, well understood the grace God had shown to him. He described in 1 Corinthians 15:9–10 how that understanding made him *much more* zealous to serve God and minister to the church, saying, "*I persecuted the church of God. But ... His grace toward me was not in vain; but I labored more abundantly than they all.*"

Chapter 13

Salvation by Grace

Who has saved us ... not according to our works,
but according to His ... grace.
—2 Timothy 1:9

We cannot do anything to cause our sins to be forgiven, to save ourselves, or to merit salvation. Rather, God must save by His grace. As it is written in 2 Timothy 1:9, "*Who has saved us ... not according to our works, but according to His own purpose and grace.*" Accordingly, Romans 3:20 informs us that "*by the works of the Law no flesh will be justified in His sight; for through the Law comes the knowledge of sin*" (NASB). And Romans 3:28 concludes from the verses preceding it, "*Then we consider a man to be justified by faith without works of law*" (ATR).

The Greek word in Romans 3:28 rendered "*consider*" at first seems unexpected. But it is fitting to say we "*consider*" it, or think of it in that way, since it is not literally the case that a man's faith justifies him. Rather, it is God who, by His grace, justifies those who have faith; and it is in that sense that they are justified by their faith.[108] The preceding verses in Romans 3:22–24 describe those details. They tell us the "*righteousness of God*" is given to "*all those who believe; for there is no distinction; for all have sinned and fall short of the glory of God, being justified as a gift by His grace*" (NASB).

---

[108] Similarly, we understand that is what was meant by Jesus' statement in Luke 7:50, "*Your faith has saved you.*" As the context there makes clear, **Jesus** saved the woman, forgiving her sins, **because** she had faith.

By His grace, God justifies the one who believes in Jesus. And so it is written in Ephesians 2:8, *"For by grace you have been saved through faith."*

In the same way, a beggar's begging does not merit nor is owed charity. Neither can it produce the things the beggar needs. However, someone might be gracious and give to a beggar. As a result, it could then be said, "By grace the beggar's needs were provided for through begging." Yes, they were provided for **through** begging. But they were provided for **by** the person who, moved with compassion, **by grace gave** what was begged.

The blind Bartimaeus knew how to beg (Mark 10:46), and he is given as an example for us. Hearing that Jesus was near, he cried out, *"Jesus, Son of David, have mercy on me"* (v. 47). By calling Jesus the Son of David, Bartimaeus expressed his faith that Jesus is the promised Messiah.

However, Jesus did not answer Bartimaeus. Nevertheless, even when *"many warned him to be quiet ... he cried out all the more"* (v. 48). For he knew that Jesus was able to give him his sight, and that if Jesus did not, he would never have it. Therefore, he cried out until Jesus stood still and called him, and in mercy gave him what he begged. Jesus told him in Mark 10:52 (which is recorded with the same five Greek words and inflections as what He spoke in Luke 7:50), *"Your faith has saved you"* (ATR).

The lyrics written in the 1700's to the hymn "Rock of Ages" poetically describe the truth that God must save us by His grace:

> Could my zeal no respite know,
> Could my tears forever flow,
> All for sin could not atone;
> Thou must save, and Thou alone.
> ... I ... Helpless, look to Thee for grace[109]

---

[109] Augustus Toplady, "Rock of Ages," 1776. Reprinted in *Trinity Hymnal*, hymn 421.

The repentant publican knew this. Unlike the Pharisee praying near him, he did not even lift his eyes toward heaven, but smote his breast while pleading, "*God, be merciful to me a sinner!*" (Luke 18:13) And God, by His grace, at the cost of the sacrifice of His Son for that man's sins, forgave him.

Chapter 14

What Grace Is

Now to him who works, the wages are not counted as grace but as debt.
—Romans 4:4

Because grace is so important, it is worth understanding well what this *grace* is by which we are saved. We would like to seek a better understanding of what God used that word to describe in the New Testament. The means used to develop a better understanding of this word can also be used to come to a better understanding of other words in the Bible.

The Greek word that has been rendered "*grace*" in all verses quoted from the New Testament in this book is the noun χάρις (Strong's #5485, transliterated here *charis*). *Charis* appears more than 150 times in the New Testament. Surprisingly, it does not appear until the book of Luke—it is not found *anywhere* in either Matthew or Mark.

The gospel of Jesus Christ is called "*the gospel of the grace of God*" in Acts 20:24, and is called "*the word of His grace*" in Acts 14:3. Yet, remarkably, grace is not commanded to be preached *by name* in the gospel. And grace is not *mentioned* by name in any of the New Testament transcripts of gospel messages that record what the apostles preached to the unsaved after Jesus was raised from the dead.[110]

---

[110] For example, Acts 10:34–43 and Acts 17:22–31.

Regrettably, the way *charis* has been rendered in some passages by many translations is a hindrance to coming to a good understanding of its meaning in the New Testament. For instance, only eleven out of twenty-six sampled English translations[111] of Romans 4:4 (quoted at the top of this chapter) rendered *charis* as *grace*. The other translations rendered *charis* as "[a] gift" (eleven of them), "a favor/favour" (three of them), and "a favor or a gift" (one). As a result, the teaching in Romans 4:4 about an important aspect of the meaning of *grace* (distinguishing it from wages owed because of someone's work) is less apparent in those fifteen other translations. In Luke 1:30, a verse examined later in this chapter that helps demonstrate what grace is, only one of those twenty-six translations rendered *charis* as *grace*.

14.1 Understanding a New Testament Word's Meaning

When trying to understand how God has used a Greek word in the New Testament—its meaning(s) in the various verses in which it appears—we naturally consider the meanings of the English word(s) that have been chosen by translators to render that Greek word in those verses.[112] We also consider the various contexts.

---

[111] The twenty-six English translations were the NKJV, NASB, LITV, YLT, ESV, KJV, ASV, NIV, NLT, English Revised Version, Berean Study Bible, Berean Literal Bible, Christian Standard Bible, Holman Christian Standard Bible, Contemporary English Version, International Standard Version, Literal Standard Version, Good News Translation, NET Bible, Amplified Bible, New Heart English Bible, God's Word Translation, NASB 1977, Douay-Rheims Bible, Weymouth New Testament, and World English Bible.

[112] There are Greek (and Hebrew) concordances of the Bible, as well as computer applications and web sites, which can show every verse in the Bible where a particular Greek (or Hebrew) word appears. They can show those verses as they have been translated in an English version of the Bible, highlighting the English word(s) that have been used to render the Greek word in each of those verses. Going "the other way," there are apps and resources (for instance, *Strong's Exhaustive Concordance* or interlinear Bibles such as Jay Green's *The Interlinear Bible*) which can show the Greek or Hebrew word behind an English word in a translation. Even those without any knowledge of biblical Greek or Hebrew can make use of the many resources which have keyed those words to Strong's numbers.

As with other words in a translation of the New Testament, the English word *grace* can have various meanings in common use that are unrelated to how God has used *charis*. To illustrate, in the first edition of Noah Webster's *An American Dictionary of the English Language*, printed in 1828, he enumerated twenty different meanings of the word *grace* when used as a noun.[113]

It is helpful to look at the definition of the word in various New Testament Greek dictionaries.[114] It is not uncommon for dictionaries to differ in their definitions of a word, so it is useful to compare the definitions in a number of them. Dictionaries may also offer definitions of a word that have not been tested by a careful and open-minded study of its use in the Bible. In the end, we should be careful to embrace only those meanings which are consistent with the word's use in the Bible.

If a word has multiple meanings, the particular meaning that is intended in a given passage needs to be inferred from the context. But when a clear meaning of a word, which is plainly used in a number of verses, fits also in a verse where other possible meanings could be contrived, it is generally better to assume that known meaning of the word in that verse as well. In the end, in every place that word appears, there should be a meaning that fits its use there, the smaller the total number of meanings the better, and there should be no passages or biblical doctrines which conflict with those meanings as they are used.

When little children are first learning a language, there is no dictionary or verbal explanation that can teach them the meanings of many words. They need to learn the language and what different words in that language mean by simply listening to how their parents

---

[113] Noah Webster, *An American Dictionary of the English Language* (New York, NY: S. Converse, 1828), Vol. 1, 93. Reprinted in *American Dictionary of the English Language* (San Francisco, CA: Foundation for American Christian Education, 1995, ISBN 0-912498-03-X).

[114] Besides biblical Greek and Hebrew dictionaries that are available in print, they can also be accessed on various web sites and in computer applications.

use those words. In the same way, we might learn what God means by a word in the New Testament by listening carefully to how our Father in heaven has used it. We might also learn what He means by observing how He has used related words—such as a root or derived word, or a related Hebrew word in the Old Testament.

However, the most important means to seek a better understanding of *anything* in the Bible have not yet been mentioned: *Pray* that God would give you an understanding, have good *reasons* for wanting that understanding, and seek it *diligently*.

We should pray that God would give us an understanding: "*For the* LORD *gives wisdom; from His mouth come knowledge and understanding*" (Prov. 2:6). When one is given a true understanding, the result is a better understanding of what the Scriptures teach—an understanding that can be **explained from**, is **consistent** with, and **better matches** what the Scriptures teach than a prior understanding. The psalmist pleaded with God in Psalm 119:18, "*Open my eyes, that I may behold wonderful things from Your law*" (NASB). Note the psalmist prayed that God would enable him to see and understand wonderful things which are **in** God's law. And we have this promise in James 1:5, "*If any of you lacks wisdom, let him ask of God, who gives to all generously and without reproach, and it will be given to him*" (NASB).

But we need to make sure we have good reasons or motivations for wanting that wisdom, for later in the book of James we are warned, "*You ask and do not receive, because you ask with wrong motives*" (James 4:3 NASB). Some common good motives are that we may know God and His good ways and be able to walk in those ways—pleasing Him.

Accordingly, Moses prayed in Exodus 33:13, "*Now therefore, I pray, if I have found grace in Your sight, show me now Your way, that I may **know You** and that I may find grace in Your sight*." The psalmist prayed that God would teach him His statutes because God is good and He does what is good: "*You are good, and do good; teach me Your statutes*" (Ps. 119:68). In verses 33–34 of the same psalm, the psalmist asked for that wisdom so that he would be able to walk in God's good ways, "***Teach me*** *the way of Your Statutes, and I* ***will keep*** *it to the end.* ***Make me understand*** *and I* ***will keep*** *Your Law, and* ***observe it*** *with the whole heart*" (LITV).

Knowing God's ways and walking in them helps the servants of the Lord accomplish their purpose to please Him that is expressed in 2 Corinthians 5:9: "*We make it our aim, whether present or absent, to be well pleasing to Him.*"

God gives knowledge and understanding to those who diligently seek it. It is written, "*You will seek Me and find Me, when you search for Me with all your heart*" (Jer. 29:13). As Jesus said, "*Seek, and you will find*" (Matt. 7:7 and Luke 11:9). When those in the synagogue at Berea heard Paul's preaching, they were "*examining the Scriptures daily to see whether these things were so*" (Acts 17:11 NASB). As a result, many of them came to know the truth and were saved, as we read in the next verse, "*Therefore many of them believed.*" God encourages us to do so in Proverbs 2:1–5, speaking to us as sons:[115]

> *My son, if you receive my words, and treasure my com-*
> *mands within you, so that you incline your ear to wisdom,*
> *and apply your heart to understanding; yes, if you cry out*
> *for discernment, and lift up your voice for understanding, if*
> *you seek her as silver, and search for her as for hidden*
> *treasures; then you will ... find the knowledge of God.*

14.2 What Grace Means in the New Testament

The English word *kindness* has one of the closest meanings to *grace* (*charis*) in the New Testament. Looking briefly at the definition of *kindness* first, will help us better understand the meaning of *grace*. And subsequently observing similarities and differences between kindness and New Testament grace will help clarify what that grace is.

A modern, first definition of the English word *kindness* from *Webster's New World Dictionary* is, "the state, quality, or habit of

---

[115] Just as He speaks to us as sons in Prov. 3:11, as explained in Heb. 12:5.

being kind."[116] *Kindness* can also refer to **acts** of kindness, or to that which is **given** by an act of kindness. That is reflected in the second definition of *kindness* from *Webster's New World Dictionary*: "kind act or treatment."

Accordingly, there is kindness, and there is "a kindness"—as used for example in, "It is a kindness I will always remember."

Here are examples of each of those meanings of *kindness*:

(1) "His kindness is well-known."
Kindness here refers to a habit of being kind.
(2a) "Your kindness enabled us to complete our journey after all."
Kindness here refers to **a particular act** of kindness.
(2b) "Thank you for your kindness, which I received in the mail yesterday."
Kindness here refers to some material **thing given by an act** of kindness.

Grace in the New Testament is similarly used in the same two or three different ways that have been described for kindness. In each place the Greek word *charis* is used, one of the following suggested meanings fits well:

> **In the New Testament, the noun *grace—charis*— means (1) a disposition to give some good or kind things that are unmerited and uncommon to a certain group, (2a) an act of grace, or (2b) that which is given by an act of grace.**

In this definition, the "**things**" one is disposed to give by grace are not necessarily material or physical things. Also, the disposition is generally to give "**some**" *particular* kinds of things to the "**certain**

---

group." Although the things given must be "**unmerited**" in order to be given by grace, there may be criteria (such as believing [Eph. 2:8], or being humble [James 4:6]) which define or limit the "**certain group**" which a particular disposition of grace embraces. Note that, as with kindness, there is grace, and there is "a grace."

Here are examples of each of those meanings of *grace* (*charis*) in the New Testament:

(1)   *"Then the angel said to her, 'Do not be afraid, Mary, for you have found favor [a regrettable rendering of the Greek word charis—grace] with God'"* (Luke 1:30). The "*grace with God*" Mary found refers to God's disposition to give Mary good or kind things that are unmerited and uncommon.

(2a) *"But as you abound in everything ... see that you abound in this grace also"* (2 Cor. 8:7). "*This grace*" refers to a particular act of grace—compiling a gift to send to the saints in Jerusalem who were in need.[117]

(2b) *"Whomever you approve ... I will send to carry your grace to Jerusalem"* (1 Cor. 16:3 LITV). The grace they would "*carry*" refers to money (or other material goods) given by acts of grace for the saints in Jerusalem.

Unobservable grace *in* a person is manifested by that person's observable acts. Observable **acts** of grace also include words a person **speaks**. Accordingly, we read from Psalm 45:2 that grace is poured upon the Messiah's lips. That means that His speech is often an act of grace—an outworking of His disposition to give good or kind things that are unmerited and uncommon.

The three meanings of *grace* can all be seen in the grace Paul had toward the believers in Corinth. Because of his grace (meaning 1) toward them, he desired to visit them so that he could help them in

---

[117] This ministry to the saints in Jerusalem is spoken about in 1 Cor. 16:1–4 and 2 Cor. 8:1–9:14.

those areas they had needs, and be able to do good to them. Therefore, his visiting them because of that grace, and the gifts they would receive because of his visiting, would be "a grace" to them (meaning 2). Paul had visited the Corinthians before writing 2 Corinthians. In that letter, he wrote of his plans to come to them again, and called the good things that they would receive from his visit "*a second grace*" (meaning 2b): "*I purposed to come to you ... that you might have a second benefit [a regrettable rendering of the Greek word charis—grace]*" (2 Cor. 1:15 LITV).

Be careful not to confuse (as many do) what grace **is** with what God has **done**, **does**, or is **able** to do **because of** His grace.[118] What God, or people, may *do* because of grace is different from what grace *means*.

14.3 Grace and Kindness

There are some important differences between kindness and grace that are reflected in these definitions. First, kindness connotes a quality of a person—something which they bring to, and influences, their interactions with all. Whereas grace is a disposition a person has toward a certain group of people. The group embraced by a particular disposition of grace could be as small as one (as in Luke 1:30, or 1 Cor. 15:10 in which Paul speaks of "*His grace toward me*") or as large as everyone (as in Matt. 5:45).

A person may have one kind of grace toward one group, and a different kind toward another. A person may have a disposition to give certain good things to one group, while other good things to another group. As mentioned previously, James 4:6 (and 1 Pet. 5:5) describes grace which God has toward the humble only, "*God sets Himself against proud ones, but He gives grace to humble ones*" (LITV).

---

[118] For example, Wigram-Green's *The New Englishman's Greek Concordance and Lexicon* gives for the definition of *grace* as a "theological technical term" on pp. 913–914, "*grace* = all that God the Father is free to do for His chosen people on the basis of His sovereignty and the finished work of Christ."

Second, grace includes what is good **or** kind. What is kind is not always good for someone.[119] And what is good for someone may not be considered kind (as something pleasant to receive or giving relief). For example, a rebuke may be good for someone, yet may not be thought of as kind.

Third, in kindness, you could give what is kind to those who are kind to you, or who are thankful or good. At times they may do some kindness to you, and at other times you show kindness to them. In kindness, you may give to those for whom it is customary to do so, or due in some manner. However, those acts do not necessarily show or evidence grace in the one doing them, because grace is a disposition to give what is both unmerited and uncommon.

An example of this aspect of New Testament grace is illustrated in a passage that records Jesus' words in Luke 6:32–35. In it, the Greek word *charis* is used three times. Here is a fairly literal translation of that passage:

> *If ye love those loving you, what grace have ye? for also the sinful love those loving them; and if ye do good to those doing good to you, what grace have ye? for also the sinful do the same; and if ye lend to those of whom ye hope to receive back, what grace have ye? for also the sinful lend to sinners—that they may receive again as much. But love your enemies, and do good, and lend, hoping for nothing again, and your reward will be great, and ye shall be sons of the Highest, because He is kind unto the ungracious and evil.* (YLT)

A disposition to give what is good or kind to a group is shown by giving some good or kind thing to them. But in this passage, Jesus taught that doing good to someone does not necessarily demonstrate the grace that God commands us to have. Jesus said, *"If ye do good to those doing good to you, what grace have ye? for also the sinful*

---

[119] For example, in Gen. 19:17–22 and 30, God spared Zoar and permitted Lot to flee there, instead of to the mountains as he had been directed to go. That was kind to Lot, though not good for him.

do the same." We could interpret Jesus' rhetorical question, *"what grace have ye?"* to be asking, "How does that act show you have grace?" The implied answer is, "It does not," and the reason Jesus gave is because *"the sinful do the same."*

In other words, doing good to those who do good to us does not show we have grace *because* the sinful often do the same thing. By definition then, grace is a disposition to do good to others beyond what the sinful often do—in an uncommon way. For example, loving your enemies and doing good to *them* shows grace. Being kind to the ungracious and evil is a kindness that rises to the level of showing grace. Those acts give what is both unmerited and uncommon.

It is written in Romans 4:3–5, *"'Abraham believed God, and it was* **counted** *to him for righteousness.' Now to one* **working**, *the reward is not* **counted** *according to grace, but [the reward is] according to* **debt**. *But to the one not working, but believing on Him justifying the ungodly, his faith is counted for righteousness"* (LITV). This passage makes explicit what should not surprise us: that giving a reward to someone to whom it is due—when *"the reward is ... according to debt"*—is not giving according to grace. Romans 11:6 comes alongside this teaching: *"And if by grace, then it is no longer of works; otherwise grace is no longer grace."* Grace gives what is unmerited.

Abraham did not have righteousness as a result of his works, nor as the reward for them, nor because of what he was due (*"according to debt"*). Neither was Abraham owed, nor did he merit, salvation because of his faith. Rather, righteousness was *"counted according to grace."* God justified Abraham by grace by **counting** righteousness to him because of his faith. To do so, the Son of God needed to be sacrificed for Abraham's sins. That gift required what **no man** could **ever** merit.

14.4 Grace and Mercy

Grace and *mercy*, though not synonymous, are often found inter-mixed in the New Testament. For instance, some particular mercy may also be an act of grace. Of course, the meanings of *grace* and *mercy* in the New Testament prescribe the way they may be inter-mixed.

Our present day meaning and use of the English word mercy is generally similar to the meaning and use of the Greek word in the New Testament that is usually rendered mercy in faithful English translations. That word is the noun ἔλεος (Strong's #1656, transliterated here *eleos*). Its related verb (to have mercy on or show mercy to) is ἐλεέω (Strong's #1653, transliterated here *eleeo*).

Mercy is a manifestation or outworking of compassion or pity. In its broadest sense, I suggest New Testament mercy, *eleos*, is "the provision of relief or deliverance from a bad situation or need, not because it is due, but because of pity or compassion." Correspondingly, the related verb *eleeo* means "to provide relief or deliverance from a bad situation or need, not because it is due, but because of pity or compassion." Frequently, mercy involves withholding or tempering some consequence or penalty that is due because of an offense. However, an offense and associated consequence do not need to be involved (as shown in Luke 10:36–37, Matt. 17:15, and Mark 10:46–47).

Mercy is a provision that is given through some action or change in action, whereas grace (in meaning 1) is a disposition. The adjective merciful can denote a disposition or quality of a person.

Grace and mercy are mentioned together in a number of passages. One of those is 1 Timothy 1:2: "*Grace, mercy, and peace from God our Father and Jesus Christ our Lord.*" By God's grace, He may have mercy. In mercy, God may give grace. Hebrews 4:16 is an example of both when it encourages us, "*Let us therefore come boldly to the throne of grace, that [because of that grace] we may obtain mercy and [as a result] find grace to help in time of need.*"

Our sins must be forgiven for us to be saved, and Romans 4:4–7 teaches us that it is by grace that God forgives our sins. But forgiving someone's sins is surely also having mercy on that person. Jesus showed that is the case when He told a parable to teach us that we ought to forgive our brothers' sins in Matthew 18:23–35. He described a king who forgave one of his slaves a great debt and said, "*I forgave you all that debt because you pleaded with me ... I had mercy on you*" (vv. 32–33 NASB).

God saves us by His grace. But Titus 3:5 says that He saves us according to His mercy: "*Not by works of righteousness which we have done, but according to His mercy He saved us.*" Those words that describe God's mercy in saving us, are almost identical to the words that describe God's *grace* in saving us in 2 Timothy 1:9: "*Who has saved us ... not according to our works, but according to His ... grace.*"

14.5 Grace and Love

Grace and *love* are also often found intermixed, though they are not synonymous. Love is often a motivation for grace (1 John 4:9). And love may be an act of grace. In the passage quoted from Luke 6 in section 14.3, Jesus commanded us to have the grace which loves our enemies. An enemy is not just someone who does not love you, but is someone who is actively against you—who seeks your harm or failure. Those who love their enemies show grace.

One way to love our enemies, and one which may result in the greatest blessing to our enemies, is to enable them to hear the gospel so that they might believe and be saved. God has made preaching the gospel—which is "*to Jews a stumbling block and to Gentiles foolishness*" (1 Cor. 1:23 NASB)—such that it often requires grace to do it. In Romans 10:21, God tells us of the grace He has had in calling people to Himself: "*All day long I have stretched out My hands to a disobedient and contrary people.*" This good which God has done for His enemies is both unmerited and uncommon. Of course, God did much more in loving His enemies than stretching out His hands, as described in John 3:16.

We can see in the description of Ephesians 2:4–5 something which should not surprise us—both **mercy** and **love** at work in God's **grace** by which we are saved: "*But God, **being** rich in mercy, **because of** His great love with which He loved us, even when we were dead in our transgressions, made us alive together with Christ (**by grace** you have been saved)*" (NASB).

14.6 What Grace Does

Grace may do good to some in a way that is clearly unmerited and uncommon by doing good to them while suffering unjustly at their hands, patiently enduring the injustice. First Peter 2:19–24 describes this grace, and an example of it which Jesus gave us:

> *For this is grace, if because of conscience of God, anyone endures griefs when suffering unjustly. For what glory [is it], if when sinning and being beaten you will patiently endure? But if when doing good and suffering you will patiently endure, this is grace before God. For to this you were called, because Christ also suffered for our sake, leaving us an example, in order that you might follow in His steps;* **who** *did no sin, nor was deceit found in His mouth;* **who** *when being reviled was not reviling in return, when suffering was not threatening, but was committing to the One judging righteously;* **who** *Himself took up* **our** *sins in His body to the tree, in order that we, after dying to sins, might live to righteousness;* **of whom** *by His bruise* **you** *were healed.* (ATR)

Consider this example Jesus left us. We are taught that it is not a glory for someone to patiently endure being beaten for sinning. Such a person is suffering justly. As one of the criminals who was crucified with Jesus said to the other criminal about what they were suffering, *"We indeed are suffering justly, for we are receiving what we deserve for our deeds"* (Luke 23:41 NASB). He then said about Jesus, *"But this man has done nothing wrong"* (NASB).

Jesus was not suffering for any wrong He had done. Unlike every other man, He never sinned in any way—ever. And He was much more than beaten, He was put to death. And He suffered not just any death, but one of the cruelest deaths ever invented. After being beaten and flogged and stripped, He was nailed to a cross on which He was hung to die. And He suffered more than the physical agony, *"for He made Him who knew no sin to be sin for us, that we might become the righteousness of God in Him"* (2 Cor. 5:21).

He endured these things in order that He might save even those who were unjustly putting Him to death. Taking up their sins along with ours in His body to the cross, He prayed, *"Father, forgive them..."* (Luke 23:34). It is written, *"For scarcely for a righteous man will one die; yet perhaps for a good man someone would even dare to die. But God demonstrates His own love toward us, in that while we were still sinners, Christ died for us. ...* **when we were enemies** *we were* **reconciled** *to God* **through** *the death of His Son"* (Rom. 5:7–8, 10)!

We are told, *"This is grace."*

Chapter 15

Finding Grace With God

Come boldly to the throne of grace, that we may ... find grace.
—Hebrews 4:16

15.1 What It Means to Find Grace With God

When God sent the angel Gabriel to Mary and he greeted her, she was troubled at his greeting. Luke 1:28–29 recounts that event: "*And having come in, the angel said to her, 'Rejoice, highly favored one, the Lord is with you; blessed are you among women!' But ... she was troubled at his saying, and considered what manner of greeting this was.*" We might expect Mary's trouble over his greeting was a feeling of "Uh oh, what is about to happen, that I'm greeted by this stranger in such an unusual manner??"

However, those things—being highly favored, the Lord being with you, being blessed among women—are surely not something to be troubled about, or to fear what might now happen to you (if you believe they are so)! Accordingly, in verse 30, the angel summarized this by telling Mary not to fear, "*for you have found favor [charis: grace] with God.*" She had nothing to fear, "*for*" she had "*found grace with God.*"

When someone has found grace with God, it means that God has a special grace toward that person—"*the Lord is with you; blessed are you.*" God had a special disposition to do good to Mary. His purposes were to be with her and bless her—in unmerited and uncommon ways! Therefore, she need not fear as to what the angel was sent to tell her, or what God would bring upon her or have her do, *whatever* that might be.

We might expect that Mary's greatest earthly hope and joy at that time was her impending marriage to Joseph, to whom she was be-trothed. But the angel told her that she would conceive in her womb by the Holy Spirit—she would become pregnant. Joseph was a right-eous man who had kept Mary's virginity. When he found out Mary was pregnant, he knew the child was not begotten by him but by someone else. And so, as Mary could have expected, he purposed to divorce her (Matt. 1:18–19). One can only imagine how difficult their conversation about this must have been, especially if they did not have that conversation until it became clear Mary was pregnant some time after she returned from her extended visit with Elizabeth of about three months (Luke 1:56).

In this case, God intervened by telling Joseph in a dream that he should not divorce her, because the child was begotten by the Holy Spirit (Matt. 1:20). There is no indication God told Mary beforehand that He would intervene in this way. And even though He did inter-vene, they both still bore the contempt of many they knew—who could only conclude they had committed fornication while they were betrothed. John 8:41 seems to indicate this story was spread widely. Yet, nevertheless, Mary well said to the angel, without fear, *"Behold, the bondslave of the Lord; may it be done to me according to your word"* (Luke 1:38 NASB).

In the same way, although God called Abraham to go out to a place *"not knowing where he was going"* (Heb. 11:8), he could go without fear, knowing he had found grace with God, and it was God's purpose to bless him (Gen. 12:1–3).

Mary soon experienced some of the great blessings of that grace she had found with God. For she exclaimed a short time later, *"All gen-erations will call me blessed. For He who is mighty has done great things for me"* (Luke 1:48–49). And what *great* things *He who is mighty* can do!

15.2 What God Can Do for Those Who Find Grace With Him

We could rather ask, what is God not able to do for those who find grace with Him—the One who is *"the God who made the world and all things in it, since He is Lord of heaven and earth"* (Acts 17:24 NASB)? Indeed, there is not anything that is too hard for Him. As Jeremiah 32:17 declares, *"Ah Lord GOD! Behold, You have made the heavens and the earth by Your great power and outstretched arm. There is nothing too hard for You."*

As described in section 12.4, God is sovereign over all that happens in His creation. God not only created us, but He also sustains us. David taught that in Psalm 3:5 when he said, *"I lay down and slept; I awoke, for the LORD sustained me."* Acts 17:25 goes further when it tells us, *"He Himself gives to all people life and breath and all things"* (NASB). He gives life as well as everything we need to live (even our breath), and everything that we have. Accordingly, God tells us in Deuteronomy 32:39, *"Now see that I, even I, am He, and there is no God besides Me; I kill and I make alive; I wound and I heal; nor is there any who can deliver from My hand."*

God knows the thoughts and intentions of our hearts (1 Sam. 16:7; Acts 1:24; 15:8; John 2:23–25). But He also exercises some power over our hearts. The Scriptures tell us that *"The king's heart is in the hand of the LORD, like the rivers of water; He turns it wherever He wishes"* (Prov. 21:1). For instance, we are told not only that Pharaoh hardened his heart (Ex. 8:15, 32, and 9:34), but that God also hardened Pharaoh's heart (Ex. 10:27, 11:10, and 14:8). In the case of Pharaoh, God said a reason He did so was *"that I may show these signs of Mine before him, and that you may tell in the hearing of your son and your son's son the mighty things I have done in Egypt, and My signs which I have done among them, that you may know that I am the LORD"* (Ex. 10:1–2).

Before sending Moses to bring His people out of Egypt, God turned the hearts of the Egyptians to hate His people and deal craftily with them (Ps. 105:25). God also kept Peter's faith from failing (Luke 22:32), and He inclined Lydia's heart to heed the things Paul was preaching when he had gone out to speak to those gathered to pray

(Acts 16:13–14).

God has power to give people over to a depraved mind, as it is written in Romans 1:28–29, "*God gave them over to a depraved mind, to do those things which are not proper, being filled with all unrighteousness*" (NASB). Since God can give someone over to a depraved mind, it follows that He is able also to give someone restraint. For to not give someone over to something, is to give that one restraint in it.

Because of this, the psalmist beseeches God, "*Turn to me and be gracious to me ... Establish my footsteps in Your word, and do not let any iniquity have dominion over me*" (Ps. 119:132–133 NASB). In the same psalm, he pleads with God, "*Make me walk in the path of Your commandments ... Incline my heart to Your testimonies ... Turn away my eyes from looking at vanity*" (vv. 35–37 NASB). And he rejoices in this hope, "*I will run the way of Your Commands, for You shall enlarge my heart*" (v. 32 LITV).

15.3 God's Grace to Believers
Hebrews 12:28 enjoins us: "*Receiving a kingdom which cannot be shaken, let us have grace, **by which** we may serve God acceptably.*" This grace refers to gifts given to us by acts of God's grace to enable us to serve Him acceptably. By His grace, God gives gifts that empower believers to accomplish things or endure trials and to live uprightly before Him.

A passage in Ephesians 4:7–13 shows that God, by His grace, gives such gifts to each believer. It begins by saying that "*to each one of us was given grace according to the measure of the gift of Christ*" (v. 7 LITV). It then goes on to give examples of some of those gifts: "*He Himself gave some to be apostles, some prophets, some evangelists, and some pastors and teachers*" (v. 11). And it lists these purposes of the gifts: "*unto the perfecting of the saints, for a work of ministration, for a building up of the body of the Christ [believers]*" (v. 12 YLT).

Paul referred to a special gift given to him by God's grace, so that he might carry out his ministry to the Gentiles, when he said, "*I was *made a minister according to the gift of the grace of God given to me, according to the working of His power* " (Eph. 3:7 LITV), and again when he spoke "*of the grace given to me by God, that I might be a minister of Jesus Christ to the Gentiles, ministering the gospel of God, that the offering of the Gentiles might be acceptable, sanctified by the Holy Spirit*" (Rom. 15:15–16).

The manifold grace of God gives diverse gifts to believers, so that they may each minister their gifts to the body of Christ for its building up. First Peter 4:10 tells us that we should be, "*each one as he received a gift, ministering it to yourselves [fellow believers] as good stewards of the manifold grace of God*" (LITV). First Corinthians 1:4–7 talks about the diverse gifts God gave by His grace to individual believers in Corinth. It says the "*grace of God which was given to you [diverse gifts given to individuals in Corinth]*," resulted in their being enriched "*in everything ... so that you are not lacking in any gift*" (LITV).

God is glorified and His power shown when He enables believers, by His grace, to accomplish things or endure trials which they do not have power to do of themselves. In 2 Corinthians 12:7–10, Paul described a painful affliction in his flesh that buffeted him, and that he earnestly entreated God to take from him.[120] But God would not remove it, but instead answered him, "*My grace is sufficient for you, for **My power** is perfected in [**your**] weakness*" (v. 9 LITV). "*Therefore*," Paul said in verse 10, "*I **take pleasure** in infirmities, in reproaches, in needs, in persecutions, in distresses, for Christ's sake. For when I am weak, then I am strong [powerful—this Greek adjective has the same root verb as the Greek noun 'power' used in v. 9].*"

Note that "sins" is missing from Paul's list, and that should be no surprise. Instead, if it were included, then Paul would be saying that

---

[120] This may refer to a health issue Paul had with his eyes, which Gal. 4:13–15 mentions and Gal. 6:11 implies. Besides other physical trials, having been stoned, lashed five times, and beaten with rods three times (2 Cor. 11:24–25), we might expect Paul to have suffered from any number of lingering physical ailments.

he takes pleasure in sinning because when he is sinning, then he is powerful![121]

Paul said in 2 Corinthians 12:7 it was because of the great revelations that were given to him that his painful affliction was also given to him to keep him from becoming proud: "*Because of the surpassing greatness of the revelations, for this reason, to keep me from exalting myself, there was given me a thorn in the flesh, a messenger of Satan to torment me—to keep me from exalting myself*" (NASB). God lets us feel our weaknesses and needs in order that we may not deceive ourselves, and our hearts be lifted up with pride, but that we may know that we depend on Him to enable us to serve Him acceptably by His grace.

And He is well able to strengthen and equip us to do His work. As Paul said, "*I can do all things through Christ who strengthens me*" (Phil. 4:13)! In Isaiah 41, God says to the seed of Abraham, "*Fear not, for I am with you; be not dismayed, for I am your God. I will strengthen you, yes, I will help you, I will uphold you ... For I, the LORD your God, will hold your right hand, saying to you, 'Fear not, I will help you*'" (vv. 10, 13).

We can see how God used an incident that is recorded in Judges 6:33–8:21 to teach Israel these things. In it, all of Midian and Amalek and the sons of the east, more than **130,000** men (Judg. 8:10), had gathered together to fight Israel. Gideon, an Israelite, assembled a comparatively small army of **32,000** (Judg. 7:3) to go out to battle them. But the Lord told Gideon that he had *too many* men in his army for the Lord to give them victory over Midian. With that many men, they might glorify themselves against God by saying that they had delivered themselves by their own power (Judg. 7:2). Therefore, the Lord reduced their number, choosing only **300** men to go out to war, so that His power in delivering them would be *undeniable* (Judg. 7:7).

---

[121] Paul told us in Rom. 3:8 that he was misrepresented by some as saying, "*Let us do evil that good may come*," and that the condemnation of those who affirm he said that will be just.

God has done something similar under the New Covenant to teach Christians these things, as described in 1 Corinthians 1:26–29:

> *For you see your calling, brothers, [observe this about your fellow Christians] that there are not many wise according to flesh, nor many powerful, not many wellborn. But God chose the foolish things of the world that the wise might be put to shame, and God chose the weak things of the world so that He might put to shame the strong things. And God chose the low-born of the world, and the despised, and the things that are not, so that He might bring to nothing the things that are, so that no flesh might glory [boast] in His presence.* (LITV)

Not everyone understands this fundamental principle—that God has chosen the weak and despised of the world so that He might put to shame the strong and esteemed of the world, in order that no one may boast in His presence.

In fact, when Herod asked *"all the chief priests and scribes of the people"* (Matt. 2:4) where the Christ was to be born, they showed that they did not understand this principle. It is true they understood the answer to Herod's question, and that the answer was given in Micah 5:2 (*"Bethlehem"*). And they thought to quote it. However, from the accurate account of what they said that is recorded in Matthew 2:6, we see a surprising error in their quotation. The error shows they did not understand that God has chosen the things that are least—the despised and rejected by the world (like the Christ[122])—over the things that are highly esteemed by the world (like themselves[123]). In their answer, they represented Micah 5:2 as saying, *"And you, Bethlehem, land of Judah, are **by no means least**..."* (Matt. 2:6 NASB). However, Micah 5:2 actually says, *"And you, Bethlehem Ephratah, **being least**..."* (LITV). What was plainly written was incomprehensible to them!

---

[122] See, for example, Isa. 53:3 and Matt. 21:42.
[123] See, for example, Luke 16:15.

15.4 The Blessing of God's Grace to His People

The blessing of God's grace toward the unworthy vessels who are His people is shown in Psalm 126. When God redeemed His people, their mouth was filled with laughter and joyful shouting (vv. 1–2). The psalm goes on to describe the reaction the nations had to His people's deliverance and joy. It was certainly *not* to rejoice over what God had done for them. It was also not to glorify God for His great works. The reaction of the nations was to scornfully sneer at God's people, saying, *"The* LORD *has done great to work* **with** ***these!"***[124] (v. 2 ATR)

The response of God's people is recorded next, in verse 3. They agreed with what the nations had said in mockery, even using identical Hebrew words up to *"with these,"* saying, *"The* LORD **has done** *great to work with us,"* and then added, ***"we are glad"*** (ATR). Although they were unworthy, and although they were scorned by the world, the Lord had done wonderfully, and worked with them, and redeemed them. And so, despite the nations' scorn, they had rejoicing and joy.

Because of God's grace, His people have true joy. When Sarah gave birth to Isaac, she rejoiced in the miracle God had performed and this astonishing gift He had given to her who had been barren, and was then about ninety years old,[125] saying, *"God has made laughter for me"* (Gen. 21:6 NASB). Then Sarah exclaimed, *"Everyone who hears will laugh with me"* (NASB). In saying that, she used the same Hebrew word for *"hear"* that is used in a passage from Isaiah 1:18–19 in which God says that those who *"are willing and hear"* (LITV) will have their sins forgiven and eat the good of the land. That same word for "hear" is also used in Isaiah 55:3: *"Incline your ear, and come to Me.* **Hear***, and your soul shall live; and I will make an everlasting covenant with you."*

Sarah was expressing that God would give that same joy He had given her, to *"everyone who hears"*—meaning, to those who are

---

[124] Note that it is *"with these,"* and not "for these" (as many translations render it).
[125] Gen. 17:17.

characterized by "hearing God." Psalm 32:10–11 describes the joy and rejoicing which those who trust in God have: "*He who trusts in the* LORD, *mercy shall surround him. Be glad in the* LORD *and rejoice, you righteous; and shout for joy, all you upright in heart!*"

As we saw in chapter 6, Romans 8:28 tells us that God's grace toward those who love Him extends much beyond the deliverances, blessings, and joys He gives them. It tells us that God works **all things** for the good of **those who love Him**—even those things which are "fiery trials." Four verses later, verse 32 explains and expounds on that further with this rhetorical question: "*He who did not spare His own Son, but delivered Him up for us all, how shall He not with Him also freely give us all things?*" Since God did not spare His own Son for us, He surely will not withhold anything else that is good for those who have now come to His Son. Accordingly, it is written in Psalm 84:11, "*The* LORD *will give grace and glory; no good thing will He withhold from those who walk uprightly.*"

First Corinthians 15:56–57 states, "*But the **sting of death**:*[126] *sin; but the **power of sin**: the **law**; but by God: **grace**—by the One [continually] giving to us the victory **through** our Lord Jesus Christ*" (ATR). By God's grace, He is continually giving us the victory, and He does so through our Lord Jesus Christ. Second Corinthians 2:14 states this same thing, and begins with the identical five Greek words found within 1 Corinthians 15:57: "*But by God: grace—by the One always leading us in triumph in Christ*" (ATR).

All those believing in our Lord Jesus Christ are blessed with this blessing, "*May **the God of all grace**, who called us to His eternal glory by Christ Jesus, after you have suffered a while, perfect, establish, strengthen, and settle you. To Him be the glory and the dominion forever and ever. Amen*" (1 Pet. 5:10–11).

---

[126] The sting of death refers to what makes death dreadful, just like the sting of a scorpion is dreadful (whose sting is mentioned in Rev. 9:5–6, 10).

Chapter 16

The Fitting and Required Response

The grace of God has appeared ... instructing us
to deny ungodliness and worldly desires.
—Titus 2:11 NASB

The grace of God has now appeared that brings salvation to all men—Jesus Christ has come in the flesh and given Himself a ransom for us. Surely, that should make us thankful and grateful. Surely, we should glorify God for His grace shown to us, praising and worshiping Him. The book of Revelation shows that will be a theme of praise and worship in heaven forever:

> *And they sang a new song, saying: "You are worthy to take the scroll, and to open its seals; for You were slain, and have redeemed us to God by Your blood out of every tribe and tongue and people and nation…" Then I looked, and I heard the voice of many angels around the throne, the living creatures, and the elders; and the number of them was ten thousand times ten thousand, and thousands of thousands, saying with a loud voice: "Worthy is the Lamb who was slain to receive power and riches and wisdom, and strength and honor and glory and blessing!"* (Rev. 5:9, 11–12)

It is recorded in Luke 17:12–19 that Jesus cleansed ten lepers who had begged Him for mercy. Jesus did not heal them immediately, but told them to go show themselves to the priests, and they were cleansed from their leprosy while they were on their way. Imagine what this meant for those lepers. Besides the physical healing of their bodies, it meant they would no longer be looked on with horror and fear, a person could touch them without being made unclean, and they could return to their loved ones, to friendships, society, etc.

However, when the lepers found that they were cleansed, *only one* of them returned to thank Jesus and give Him glory! We are told in verses 15–16, "*And one of them having seen that he was healed did turn back, with a loud voice glorifying God, and he fell upon his face at his feet, giving thanks to him, and he was a Samaritan*" (YLT). This prompted Jesus to then ask not one but three consecutive rhetorical questions in verses 17–18: "*Were there not ten cleansed? But where are the nine? Were there not any found who returned to give glory to God except this foreigner?*"[127] The thanklessness of those nine is both offensive and unrighteous, and these things are certainly intended to instruct and warn us.

Let us not be as the one "*having become forgetful of the cleansing of his old sins*" (2 Pet. 1:9 YLT). Let us never forget God's great grace toward us and cease to glorify and thank Him for it.

Titus 2:11–14 summarizes some other important things we are taught by God's grace in bringing in the New Covenant:

> For **the grace of God** has appeared, bringing salvation to all men, **instructing us** to deny ungodliness and worldly desires and to live sensibly, righteously and godly in the present age, looking for the blessed hope and the appearing of the glory of our great God and Savior, Christ Jesus, who gave Himself for us to redeem us from every lawless deed, and to purify for Himself a people for His own possession, **zealous** for good deeds. (NASB)

---

[127] Verse 19 shows us the underlying reason the Samaritan man returned while the others did not: He had faith. A literal translation of that verse also indicates that this one who returned then received much more from the Savior, and something which the passage does not say the others received. For Jesus said to him, "*Thy faith hath saved thee*" (YLT).

16.1 Seek to Be Holy in All Your Behavior

Hebrews 12:14 exhorts us to "*pursue ... holiness, without which no one will see the Lord.*" The first chapter of 1 Peter describes some important New Testament context in which this command to pursue holiness is given. It begins by speaking about the salvation God has now provided through the sufferings and resurrection of Jesus Christ. It tells us that the prophets in the Old Testament prophesied of this salvation and grace God has now brought to us in these latter days: "*Of **this salvation** the prophets have inquired and searched carefully, who prophesied of **the grace that would come to you** ... To them it was revealed that, not to themselves, but to us they were ministering the things which now have been reported to you through those who have preached the gospel to you*" (vv. 10, 12).

The next verse of this passage starts with "***Therefore***," and it begins a description of the response we should have to this salvation and grace. Verse 14 charges us to be "*as obedient children, do not be conformed to the former lusts which were yours in your ignorance*" (NASB), and verse 15 commands, "*Like the Holy One who called you, be holy yourselves also in all your behavior*" (NASB).

The verses in 1 Peter which follow expand on some reasons for being holy in all our behavior: "*Because it is written, 'You shall be holy, for I am holy.' ... knowing that you were not redeemed with perishable things like silver or gold from your futile way of life inherited from your forefathers, but with precious blood, as of a lamb unblemished and spotless, the blood of Christ*" (vv. 16, 18–19 NASB).

Verse 16 quotes from Leviticus 11:45. In it, God says we should be holy because He is holy: "***for** I am holy.*" He is speaking here to those who "*address [Him] as Father*" (v. 17 NASB), whom He has called on to be "*as obedient children*" in verse 14. Because God is holy, so also His children should be holy.

Another reason given we should be holy in all our behavior is because of "***knowing that** you were ... redeemed ... with precious blood ... the blood of Christ.*" In order to redeem us by His grace, to forgive our sins and deliver us from so great a death, the Son of God needed to "*[take] up our sins in His body to the tree*" (1 Pet. 2:24 ATR), to be "*made ... sin for us*" (2 Cor. 5:21), to "*become a curse for us*" (Gal. 3:13), and to give Himself a sacrifice for our sins (Eph. 5:2). Then, "*knowing that*," to do *other* than seek to be holy in all our behavior (that is, to go on willfully in any of those sins) is to despise God's grace to us and trample on the Son of God (as described in section 11.2).

The hymn "When I Survey the Wondrous Cross" expresses it, "Love so amazing, so divine, demands my soul, my life, my all."[128] Romans 12:1 calls on us to "*present your bodies a living sacrifice, holy, acceptable to God, which is your reasonable service.*"

This is a fitting response, which we are required to seek.

16.2 Have and Grow in Grace
We should not only stand in awe of God's grace, thanking and praising Him for it, but we should also have and grow in grace. For Colossians 4:6 instructs us, "*Let your speech always be with grace*," and 2 Peter 3:18 commands us to "*grow in grace*" (LITV).

This should not surprise us, for Jesus said, "*A disciple is not above his teacher, but everyone who has been perfected will be like his teacher*" (Luke 6:40 LITV). Because Jesus has grace, we should also.

We are told in 1 John 2:6, "*The one who says he abides in Him ought himself to walk in the same manner as He walked*" (NASB), and in 1 John 4:17, "*By this, love has been perfected with us ... that as He is, we are also in this world*" (LITV). The general principle taught in those passages is that we should strive to become like our Lord Jesus in all His ways.

The passage from Luke 6:32–35 discussed in section 14.3 described grace we should have. In it, Jesus taught that because our Father in heaven is kind to the ungracious and evil, we should be also. He said

---

[128] Isaac Watts, "When I Survey the Wondrous Cross," 1709. Reprinted in *Trinity Hymnal*, hymn 186.

that those who do "*shall be sons of the Highest, because He is kind unto the ungracious and evil*" (Luke 6:35 YLT).

God has grace; therefore also, so should those who are His children.

16.3 Speak With Grace

We read in Colossians 4 that our speech should always be with grace, but what does that mean? Since grace is poured upon Jesus' lips (Ps. 45:2), His speech provides perfect examples for us to learn from. The instruction in Colossians 4:6 more fully says, "*Let your speech always be with grace, seasoned with salt, that you may know how you ought to answer each one.*"

Speech that is "*with grace*" is **speech that is shaped by** a disposition to impart something good or kind that is unmerited and uncommon. Note that such speech, which should be "*seasoned with salt,*" may not always be perceived as pleasant or "gracious" (as that word is used in modern English).

According to the definitions of New Testament grace given earlier, the good gift one hopes to impart to those who hear such speech can also be called grace. Ephesians 4:29 uses *grace* in that way when it tells us, "*Let ... proceed out of your mouth ... what is good for necessary edification, that it may* **impart grace** *to the hearers.*" In this verse, "*necessary edification*" is the good gift one hopes to impart. It is only that it "*may*" be imparted since it would clearly *not* be imparted if the hearers reject what is said. But if the hearers receive that "*necessary edification,*" then **that grace**—specifically the **gift** of the **necessary** edification—was imparted to them by the speaker's act of grace (the speaker's speech).

As described in section 14.5, God has made preaching the gospel such that it often requires grace. Preaching the gospel usually does not ingratiate oneself with the world, but can result in everything from covert discrimination to open animosity and violence.[129]

---

[129] There is a time when speaking is not useful, and it is good to refrain from speaking (Luke 22:67–68). We should generally refrain from preaching the gospel in a situation where we perceive that none of those hearing it

Because of Paul's preaching the gospel, he endured suffering of all kinds—he was beaten, imprisoned, and stoned (Acts 14:19). This was certainly no surprise to him, because he was well aware of what he himself had done to Christians before he had seen the resurrected Jesus and believed (1 Cor. 15:8–9; Acts 7:58; Gal. 1:13). Also, the Holy Spirit did not hide from him what awaited as he traveled to preach the gospel: "*The Holy Spirit testifies in every city, saying that chains and tribulations await me*" (Acts 20:23).

Paul's preaching the gospel in those cities, so that some might hear and be saved, was speaking with grace.

16.4 Have Grace When Suffering

A passage in 1 Peter 2:19–24 (quoted in section 14.6) talks about a special kind of grace Christians should have: a disposition to endure patiently with grace situations in which they suffer unjustly. It tells us that Christians were *called* to this: "*But if when doing good and suffering you will patiently endure, this is grace before God. For to this you were called, because Christ also suffered for our sake, leaving us an example, in order that you might follow in His steps*" (vv. 20–21 ATR). We are not called to *seek* to suffer unjustly; but we are called to endure with patience situations in which we *will* suffer unjustly. And in those situations, we should do good—even to those by whose hands we suffer.

That is what Jesus did when He suffered for our sake. And the passage instructs us that Christ left us this example "*in order that you might follow in His steps*." The verse just prior to that passage speaks of the case of a Christian slave who has a harsh master, while the second verse that follows the passage speaks of the case of a Christian woman married to a man who disobeys God's word.

Later in that same book, 1 Peter 4:12–14 forewarns and encourages us about such suffering we may face: "*Beloved, do not be surprised*

---

would benefit from it, but they would only be provoked to hostility (Matt. 7:6). Nevertheless, there are situations like that in which it may be God's will for us to speak to have a testimony. For examples of this, see Matt. 10:18–19 and the account of Stephen's testimony in Acts 7.

at the fiery ordeal among you, which comes upon you for your testing, as though some strange thing were happening to you; but to the degree that you share the sufferings of Christ, keep on rejoicing ... If you are reviled for the name of Christ, you are blessed" (NASB). Philippians 1:29 explains, *"For to you it has been **granted** on behalf of Christ, not only to believe in Him, but also to suffer for His sake."* And 1 Peter 3:9 tells us how we ought to behave when treated wrongfully—not returning evil for evil, or reviling for reviling, but rather returning *blessing* for evil and reviling, because that is a means by which we *inherit blessing*: *"knowing that **you were called to this** in order that you might **inherit blessing**"* (LITV).

Three important reasons we should patiently endure with grace when suffering unjustly are found in this short phrase from 1 Peter 2:21: *"Because Christ also suffered [with grace] for our sake"* (ATR).

The Christ Suffered

A first reason is because the Christ suffered. Since it was God's will that the Son of God suffer, it should be no great surprise if it is God's will for us to suffer. When we *expect* God to bring us into situations in which it is His will that we suffer unjustly, that will help us endure those situations with grace when they occur (John 16:1–2). In fact, we are taught to **arm ourselves** with that mindset in 1 Peter 4:1: *"Therefore, since Christ suffered for us in the flesh, arm yourselves also with the same mind."* When Peter had formerly expressed the wrong idea that it could *not* be God's will that His only-begotten Son suffer in that way, Jesus gave him the sternest rebuke of any of His followers!

The incident in which Peter was rebuked is described in Matthew 16:21–22. When Jesus began to tell his disciples it was necessary for Him to go to Jerusalem, and suffer many things, and be killed, Peter objected, *"Lord! This shall never happen to **You**"* (v. 22 NASB). But Jesus said to him, *"Get behind Me, Satan! ... for you are not mindful of the things of God, but the things of men"* (v. 23). In Peter's promoting such an idea, that God would never require such a thing of

His Son, he was acting like Satan by putting a stumbling block in front of Jesus—in the path He needed to walk in order to do the will of His Father. The quotes we have seen from Peter in this section show that he truly received Jesus' correction well!

Peter's incorrect idea would be a stumbling block to *anyone* desiring to follow Jesus whom God brings into a situation in which that person will suffer. It tempts us to take offense at such a *"fiery ordeal"* and to be indignant about our treatment—as if *we* should never be subjected to sufferings like those God required His Son to endure. That incorrect idea might also seem to justify threatening, reviling, and cursing the ones who are ill-treating us, instead of patiently enduring the suffering with grace.

Further, we read in Hebrews 5:8–9 that the Son of God *"learned obedience from the things which He suffered. And having been made perfect, He became to all those who obey Him the source of eternal salvation"* (NASB). A similar statement is made in Hebrews 2:10, *"For it was fitting ... to perfect the author of their salvation through sufferings"* (NASB). These surprising statements teach us that suffering was a means by which the One who never disobeyed[130] learned obedience, and the One who is perfect was perfected!

They could be interpreted that Jesus personally experienced, as a man, the costs obedience can exact. And He experienced how a man may be able to, and with what manner and attitude he ought to, obey while bearing suffering.[131] Hebrews 2:18 tells us that because Jesus suffered in the flesh, He is able to help us in our trials: *"For in what He has suffered, being tried, He is able to help those being tried"* (LITV).

Jesus' willing obedience in the face of suffering was well pleasing to His Father. We can see this from His statement in John 10:17, *"For this reason the Father loves Me, because I lay down My life"*

---

[130] As shown by Heb. 4:15, John 8:29, and 1 Pet. 2:22.

[131] According to this interpretation of those surprising statements, we do not "learn" obedience when we are commanded to do something we wanted to do anyway.

(NASB). We are told about this obedience, and the Father's response, in Philippians 2:8–9: "*Being found in appearance as a man, He humbled Himself and became obedient to the point of death, even the death of the cross. **Therefore** God also has highly exalted Him and given Him the name which is above every name.*"

Since suffering was necessary for *Jesus'* perfection as a man, how much more then might suffering be necessary for us? The psalmist's experience agrees, for he said, "*It is good for me that I was afflicted, that I may learn Your statutes*" (Ps. 119:71 NASB), and, "*Before I was afflicted I went astray, but now I keep Your word*" (v. 67 NASB).

He Showed Us How We Ought to Endure Suffering

A second reason is because *in* Jesus' suffering unjustly, He showed us how we ought to walk in such a situation—which is with grace and patient endurance. How Jesus walked in the days of his flesh is the perfect example for us. As quoted earlier in this chapter, Jesus said, "*A disciple ... who has been perfected will be like his teacher*" (Luke 6:40 LITV). Because Jesus suffered unjustly, He did not just teach us, but showed us how we ought to walk in that situation. And in leaving this example, He left no question that we should endure unjust suffering with grace toward those treating us unjustly.

The passage from 1 Peter 2 tells us that Jesus' purpose in taking "*up our sins in His body to the tree*" was "*in order that we, after dying to sins, might live to righteousness*" (ATR). Jesus knew that by His becoming a curse (as Gal. 3:13 describes what happened when Jesus was crucified for us), His enemies could be blessed—they could be forgiven their sins and live to righteousness. Because of this, He desired to be made that curse.

Paul expressed that same desire, and his heart's great sorrow for the Jewish people who were unbelieving, in Romans 9:2–3: "*I have great sorrow and continual grief in my heart. For I could wish that I myself were accursed from Christ for my brethren, my countrymen according to the flesh.*" Because of that, Paul did not shrink back from preaching the gospel so that some might be saved, even though the consequences to him were suffering, imprisonment, and being put to death.

For example, the prophet Agabus prophesied to Paul that if he went to Jerusalem, he would be bound. And when those who were traveling with Paul heard this, they *"pleaded with him not to go up to Jerusalem"* (Acts 21:12). But Paul answered, *"What do you mean by weeping and breaking my heart? For I am ready not only to be bound, but also to die at Jerusalem"* (v. 13).

In the same way that Jesus prayed for those who were putting Him to death, Stephen followed in the steps of his Lord when he was stoned—kneeling down and crying out with a loud voice the desire of his heart: *"Lord, do not charge them with this sin"* (Acts 7:60).

He Suffered for Us

A third reason to have grace when suffering unjustly found in that short phrase from 1 Peter 2:21 is because it was for us that the Christ suffered. It does not state only that He suffered, but that He *"suffered for our sake"* (ATR). First Peter 3:18 summarizes the purpose of His suffering that was described in 1 Peter 2, *"the just for the unjust, that He might bring us to God."* By His grace, the Son of God suffered unjustly for us so that we could be forgiven and reconciled to God. In the paradoxes of God, through Jesus' unjust suffering on the cross, we can be spared an eternity of justly suffering for our sins.[132]

---

[132] In the wisdom of God, there are a number of paradoxes in Jesus' dying for our sins. Some of these are expressed well in the hymn "His Be the Victor's Name":

By weakness and defeat,
He won a glorious crown
Trod all our foes beneath His feet,
By being trodden down.
…
Made sin, He sin o'erthrew
Bowed to the grave, destroyed it so,
And death by dying slew.

Given that, how could we be so unashamed as to complain about or object to the need to endure patiently with grace a situation in which we must momentarily *"share the sufferings of Christ"* (1 Pet. 4:13 NASB)?

16.5 Have Grace Because of Grace

The last reason that was given in the previous section is perhaps the most obvious reason we should have grace—because of God's great grace toward us. Jesus demonstrated that reason by telling a parable (recorded in Matt. 18:23–35, and mentioned in section 14.4) about a king who by grace had mercy, and forgave one of his slaves a great debt that he would never have been able to repay. He forgave him because his slave fell down and begged him. But that slave later refused to forgive a fellow slave's debt, who pleaded with him in the same manner that he had previously begged the king. Although the fellow slave's debt to him was not insignificant, by comparison to all he had owed the king it was *very* little. When the king was told about it, he said to that slave he had forgiven, *"Should you not also have had mercy on your fellow slave, in the same way that I had mercy on you? And his lord, moved with anger, handed him over to the torturers"* (vv. 33–34 NASB).

The king's slave had, in effect, despised the grace and mercy which the king had shown to him by not then having mercy on his fellow slave. The righteous response of the king was to deliver him to the torturers, having decided not to forgive his great debt after all. Jesus told that parable to help His disciples understand His teaching in verse 35: *"My heavenly Father will also do the same to you, if each of you does not forgive his brother from your heart"* (NASB).

When the king asked his slave, *"Should you not also have had mercy*

Bless, bless the Conquer'r slain,
Slain in His victory;
Who lived, Who died, Who lives again—
For thee, His church, for thee!

Samuel Whitlock Gandy, "His Be the Victor's Name," 1838. Reprinted in *Hymns of Worship and Remembrance* (Belle Chasse, LA: Truth and Praise, Inc., 1950), hymn 64.

on your fellow slave, in the same way that I had mercy on you?" he expressed in that rhetorical question what is self-evident. When such great mercy has been shown to a man, he ought himself to be merciful to others. Even a Pharisee knew the answer to Jesus' question to him in Luke 7:40–43 about who would love most, one forgiven little or one forgiven much.

We who have had such great grace and mercy shown to us, should ourselves show grace and mercy to others.

Chapter 17

Conclusion

God ... now commands all men everywhere to repent.
—Acts 17:30

For the grace of God has appeared,
bringing salvation to all men.
—Titus 2:11 NASB

As indicated in the dedication, I wrote this book for those who earnestly seek the God of the Bible. By definition, they earnestly read and study the word of God so that they may know God. If you are one who does, or want to be, may God cause His face to shine on you, and be gracious to you, and lead you in paths of truth.

I have tried to express what the Bible teaches without using denominational jargon, but rather the words of the Scriptures themselves. You may have encountered descriptions in this book of some familiar biblical truths that were expressed in somewhat unfamiliar ways. If, on examining those descriptions, you found they are indeed correct and biblical, presumably they are not a stumbling block to you. Hopefully, you have appreciated them, and perhaps some have even promoted a better understanding of something you knew.

It is possible you encountered descriptions of some passages that, although appearing reasonable, contradict an understanding you have previously developed. Appendix B, "Reconciling Beliefs With Conflicting Scripture," gives helpful advice for someone who is trying to resolve an apparent conflict between what one has believed and what a "newly-noticed" passage appears to teach.

I hope that you have both a clear and precise understanding of what repentance and grace are in the New Testament. You should see the tremendous importance repentance and grace each have, and their special emphasis under the New Covenant.

It is in these latter days, through the sacrifice of the Son of God for our sins, that *"the grace of God has appeared, bringing salvation to all men"* (Titus 2:11 NASB). As we are told in John 1:17, *"The law was given through Moses, but grace and truth came through Jesus Christ."* How great a salvation we are now offered through *"the gospel of the grace of God"* (Acts 20:24)! According to that gospel, God saves all those who come to Jesus, and people come to Jesus by believing in Him and repenting from their sins.

Contrary to what many mistakenly think, this great salvation provided by God's grace gives us *more* reason to repent. Accordingly, God ushered in the New Covenant with the preaching of *"Repent"*—which is both the first word of preaching in the New Testament and the first word of Jesus' recorded preaching. Paul's final words of preaching to the Athenians recorded in Acts 17:30–31 are of ultimate importance to everyone living today: *"God ... now commands all men everywhere to repent, because He has appointed a day on which He will judge the world in righteousness by the Man whom He has ordained. He has given assurance of this to all by raising Him from the dead."*

God will not save any who have not truly believed in Jesus and repented. You should understand what it means to believe in Jesus, and the mindset of true faith. Those who truly believe in Jesus believe whatever they *understand* Jesus has said, and have a mindset to believe whatever they *may come to* understand He has said. True faith in Jesus includes a mindset to *rely on* what He has said—to trust in Him. That mindset impels one to *resolve* to follow Him—that is, to repent. Because it is a true resolve, those who are repentant also *seek* to follow Him.

As we must come to Jesus in faith and repentance to be saved, so we must continue in faith and repentance to inherit eternal life. Yet, through the Good Shepherd's shepherding, Jesus will keep all whom He has saved until He comes again—"*He who has **begun** a good work in you **will complete it** until the day of Jesus Christ*" (Phil. 1:6).

Finally, my hope is that you have seen *how* the Bible teaches and proves these simple things without contradiction, so that you may not be led astray by persuasive words. Rather, I hope that you will be able to discern the errors in arguments raised against them, and be able to give an answer from the Scriptures, with gentleness and patience, "*in meekness teaching those who have opposed, if perhaps God may give them repentance for a full knowledge of the truth*" (2 Tim. 2:25 LITV).

Chapter 18

A Conversation Unto Life

He said to them, "… that repentance and remission of sins
should be preached in His name."
—Luke 24:46–47

The following page outlines a helpful conversation you might have with some who indicate they believe in Jesus, but, for whatever reason, you are not certain they understand we must repent to be forgiven and saved. It is patterned after a conversation in Acts 19:1– 7 that Paul had with some disciples he found. As he spoke with them, he apparently began to wonder whether they fully understood the gospel. Caring for their souls, his uncertainty led him to ask about their understanding.

"I'm a Christian too!" someone says.

You ask, "When you believed, did you understand you need to repent to be saved?"

"No"   "Yes"

You show from the Scriptures our need to repent to be saved by grace.

You ask, "Do you know what it means to repent?"

You speak together about repentance—that it is a resolve to follow Jesus.

Epilogue

And he shall bring forth the capstone with shouts of
"Grace, grace to it!"
—Zechariah 4:7

Jesus said, "*I am ... the First and the Last*" (Rev. 22:13). Observe the marvelous fact that the name of Jesus, at which "*every knee should bow, of those in heaven, and of those on earth, and of those under the earth*" (Phil. 2:10), is both the first and last name in the New Testament—appearing in its first and last verses: Matthew 1:1 and Revelation 22:21.

Knowing that God has both chosen and ordered all the words in the Scriptures, and having observed that the first word of preaching in the New Testament is "*Repent*," we are interested to see God's final word to us in the Bible. And we rejoice to see that He has blessed us with this blessing in the last verse: "*The grace of our Lord Jesus Christ be with you all. Amen*" (Rev. 22:21).

Although that verse may look quite ordinary, as we might expect of God's final word to us in the Bible, it has some extraordinary aspects. To begin with, setting aside the specific mention "*of our Lord Jesus Christ*," it is surprising to find that this blessing of grace is unique to the New Testament—such a blessing is **nowhere** to be found in any Old Testament verse! For example, there is no verse in the Old Testament with the blessing "*Grace be with you*" (Col. 4:18) or "*Grace to you*" (Rom. 1:7).[133]

---

[133] Observe that the statement or promise in Ps. 84:11, "*The LORD will give grace and glory*," is not such a blessing. [Similarly, the statement or promise in 2 John 3 is not such a blessing.] The Hebrew noun for *grace* that

179

It is fitting for the Bible to end with and underscore this blessing that is unique to the New Testament. In the New Testament, we find a blessing of grace in thirty or thirty-one other verses. (I give this range because the Greek text that was used by the NASB translation does not contain the blessing in Rom. 16:24, although it does have the similar one in Rom. 16:20).

Some other surprising things are revealed by looking at two common but distinctive words in the Revelation 22:21 blessing: *grace* and *with*.[134] There are other Greek words rendered *with*, but the particular word for *with* found in Revelation 22:21 is μετά (Strong's #3326, transliterated here *meta*). Of the thirty or thirty-one other verses that have a blessing of grace, only fourteen or fifteen of them contain both *charis* and *meta* (*grace* and *with*) in any order or any position. All of those verses are in the epistles. One of them appears at the end of Hebrews, and the others appear at the end of all, but only, Paul's epistles (that is, in each of Romans through Philemon).

The blessing of grace that appears at the end of 2 Thessalonians is especially interesting. One reason is that *its* blessing in Greek is letter for letter identical to the blessing in Revelation 22:21 (in the Textus Receptus). Another reason is what Paul says in that passage containing the blessing: *"The salutation of Paul with my own hand, which is a sign in every epistle; so I write. The grace of our Lord Jesus Christ be with you all. Amen"* (2 Thess. 3:17–18).

The passage in 2 Thessalonians tells us a sign was given in every

---

is found in Ps. 84:11, and will soon be spoken of in more detail, is from the Hebrew verb חָנַן (Strong's #2603, transliterated here *chanan*). There are three blessings in the Old Testament involving the verb *chanan*: Joseph's blessing of Benjamin in Gen. 43:29, the blessing with which Aaron and his sons were instructed to bless the children of Israel in Num. 6:23–26, and a form of that blessing which the psalmist pleads with God for and/or blesses us with in Ps. 67:1.

[134] In the Rev. 22:21 blessing, *"be"* is implicit, and *"you,"* which is present in the Textus Receptus, is not in the Greek text that was used by the NASB translation, and is replaced with "the saints" in the Majority Text, as indicated in the NKJV's footnote for this verse (Nashville, TN: Thomas Nelson, 2017, ISBN 978-0-7180-9563-5), 1901.

epistle Paul wrote. Therefore, that sign would confirm an epistle was from him. He appears to tell us that he personally wrote the salutation in all of his epistles. If that is a correct understanding, then an epistle that claimed to be from Paul, but had a closing greeting[135] that was not in his handwriting, could not be from him. Of course, any *copy* made of an epistle would not have (or retain) such a sign.

However, we have just seen that the salutation itself is a sign in Paul's epistles. All of the epistles in the Bible which internally assert they are from Paul (and all of those that do, do so in their very first word) have that peculiar blessing of grace in their salutations. Amazingly, it is a blessing which, even though it appears in many varied and simple ways (using the common but distinctive words *grace* and *with*), is essentially found nowhere else in the Scriptures. This last attribute of the blessing could be given only by the Author of the entire Bible—since it depends not only on what is written in Paul's epistles, but also in every other book.

The psalmist pleaded in Psalm 119:18, *"Open my eyes, that I may behold wonderful things from Your law"* (NASB). Although the Old Testament has no verses with a blessing of grace, when we look for *any* verses in it which have both of the common but distinctive words *grace* and *with*, we indeed see wonderful things!

In the Old Testament, the Hebrew noun חֵן (Strong's #2580, transliterated here *chen*) is used for *grace*, and appears sixty-nine times. The Hebrew preposition עִם (Strong's #5973, transliterated here *im*) is used for *with*, and appears thousands of times. However, only five verses have **both** *chen* and *im*—*grace* and *with*—appearing in them in any order or position. And of those five verses, only three refer to **God's** grace.

We will look at those three verses, taking them in the order they

---

[135] This *"salutation,"* or greeting, is Strong's #783. Its related verb, "greet," is Strong's #782. Those Greek words appear more than 50 times in the epistles, but *only* at their end (except for Heb. 11:13, where it is used differently—not as a greeting between people). Hence, it is a closing greeting.

come in the Bible. Interestingly, all three mention finding grace in God's sight. And there is a remarkable relationship between the first two and the message the angel gave to Mary: that *she* had found grace with God and would give birth to that Holy One who would be called the Son of God. To make plain the criteria that (only) those three verses meet, the English words that were used in them to translate *chen* and *im* are bolded.

The first verse is Exodus 33:12: "*Then Moses said to the* LORD, '*See, You say to me,* "*Bring up this people.*" *But You have not let me know whom You will send* **with me** *[im, inflected immi]. Yet You have said,* "*I know you by name, and you have also found* **grace** *in My sight.*"'" In this verse, Moses pleaded with God: If he truly had found grace in God's sight, then whom would God send with him so that he *could* bring God's people into the promised land? Moses was well aware that, alone, he would not even have been able to "*bring up this people*" out of Egypt.

We encounter the second of the three verses as Moses continued to make the case for his cause. He said in Exodus 33:16, "*For how then will it be known that Your people and I have found* **grace** *in Your sight, except You go* **with us** *[im, inflected immanu]?*" The verb rendered "*go*" in this verse is Strong's #3212. Strong's first definition of it is "to walk."[136] Said another way, Moses asked, "How will it be known we have found grace unless You, God, walk with us?"

Observe that the inflected word rendered "*with us*" is **immanu**. Its Hebrew characters are identical to the first part of the Hebrew name (**Immanu**el) that was given to the Son whose virgin conception and birth was prophesied as a sign in Isaiah 7:14. The second part of that Son's name is the Hebrew word for *God*, which is transliterated *El* (Immanu**el**).

Isaiah 7:14 holds a special place of honor as the first passage from the Old Testament that is quoted in the New Testament. The first

---

[136] Strong, *Dictionary of the Hebrew Bible*, 49. For instance, it is rendered *walk* in Deut. 5:33.

chapter of Matthew describes the fulfillment of that prophecy in Isaiah 7:14. Matthew 1:23 quotes it and says of that Hebrew name: "*'Immanuel,' which is translated, 'God with us.'*"

Answering to Moses' plea in the two verses from Exodus, it is now known that we have found grace in God's sight because He has become flesh—Immanuel—and **God walks with us**. We can see then that these two verses point to this grace that God would bring in these latter days through our Lord Jesus Christ! He has surely brought forth the head stone with shouts of "Grace, grace!"

The third and final verse is Judges 6:17: "*Then he said to Him, 'If now I have found favor [chen—grace] in Your sight, then show me a sign that it is You who talk with me.'*" In the process of looking at what these three verses might show, and observing these things, when I came to this verse last, I was overwhelmed with the impression that in them God has given those who have found grace in His sight yet another sign that it is indeed He who talks with us in the Scriptures. We will never plumb the depths of the riches of the wisdom of God (Rom. 11:33).

The end of the matter is this: God has blessed us with this blessing, "*The grace of our Lord Jesus Christ be with you all. Amen*" (Rev. 22:21). Then, let us serve Him with joy and with the grace He supplies. For, our God is with us!

Appendix A

John's Gospel and Acts 16:31

The entirety of Your word is truth.
—Psalm 119:160

The chapter "What About John's Gospel?" summarily addressed the specific argument that it cannot be necessary to repent to be saved if the message of repentance does not appear in John's Gospel. That chapter also suggested, and tested, a reason the specific words *repent* and *repentance* were left out of John. In this appendix, we will examine in detail the reasoning in the example argument that was quoted from Hodges. In doing so, we will also look more closely at Acts 16:31 (in which *repentance* is not mentioned).

It is not that anything more needs to be said to address the argument itself. Any argument that we should set aside clear, biblical teaching because some part of the Bible is silent on that teaching should be dismissed out of hand. However, examining Hodges' reasoning is helpful to refine an understanding of some concepts, and expound on principles, that should be generally applied when trying to understand what God has written to us in the Bible.

For convenience, the statements quoted from Hodges' argument are repeated here:[137]

> The fourth evangelist explicitly claims to be doing evange-
> lism (John 20:30-31). ... Clearly, the message of John's

---

[137] Zane Hodges, *Absolutely Free! A Biblical Reply to Lordship Salvation*, 2nd ed., 130–131.

Gospel is complete and adequate without any reference to repentance whatsoever. ... The fourth gospel says nothing at all about repentance, much less does it connect repentance in any way with eternal life. ... Only a resolute blindness can resist the obvious conclusion: *John did not regard repentance as a condition for eternal life.* If he had, he would have said so. After all, that's what his book is all about: obtaining eternal life (John 20:30-31). [Italics his.]

We will take a close look at each of these statements in the order they are reasoned.

"The fourth evangelist explicitly claims to be doing evangelism (John 20:30-31)."
Calling John an "evangelist" implies he would be "doing evangelism." Calling him the "fourth" evangelist implies that the three Gospels preceding his in the New Testament—Matthew, Mark, and Luke—were also "doing evangelism." Indeed, Mark's Gospel begins with these words, *"The beginning of the gospel of Jesus Christ, the Son of God"* (Mark 1:1 NASB). The quoted statement asserts that John's Gospel "explicitly claims" to be doing evangelism in John 20:30–31.

Evangelism is a very broad term. John 20:31 describes a specific, special purpose of the book, and then gives a reason for that purpose. It says, *"These are written that you may believe that Jesus is the Christ, the Son of God, and that believing you may have life in His name."* The **special purpose** is so that readers may believe that Jesus is the Christ, the Son of God. And of course the **reason** is so that they may be saved.

Because of that special purpose, John's Gospel has much teaching about **who Jesus is** and **evidence** for that. As a result, many of the passages in the Bible which show that Jesus is God are found in John's Gospel (for instance, John 1:1 and 20:28–29, which "happen" to be the first and last verses in John prior to the referenced John 20:30–31).

Section 3.3, "Faith and Repentance in Salvation," described a special emphasis of each of the four Gospels, and how those emphases and their ordering neatly combine to present the gospel.

"Clearly, the message of John's Gospel is complete and adequate without any reference to repentance whatsoever."
What is true is that those things which John's Gospel tells us are communicated fully as God desired without ever using the words *repent* and *repentance*, for the Holy Spirit spoke through John.[138] Although its special **purpose** is that readers "*may believe that Jesus is the Christ, the Son of God*," it communicates *many* messages while carrying out that purpose, as well as messages related to other purposes. Clearly, there is *not* only one message communicated in the twenty-one chapters of John's Gospel.

Also contrary to what is asserted in the quoted statement, John is neither "complete" nor "adequate" in any of its teaching. For 2 Timothy 3:15 does not say, "you know the **Gospel of John**, that being able to make you wise to salvation through belief in Christ Jesus," but rather, "*you know the **Holy Scriptures**, those being able to make you wise to salvation through belief in Christ Jesus*" (LITV). Like every other book in the Bible, John's Gospel is augmented by, and must be interpreted in the context of, all other books in the Bible. And anything in it that is properly interpreted will not conflict with anything properly understood in those other books. For "*the entirety of Your word is truth*" (Ps. 119:160).

All together, the books of the Bible are "complete and adequate," but no book is so by itself. As it is written in Isaiah 28:9–10, "*To whom shall He teach knowledge? And to whom shall He explain the message? ... For precept must be on precept, precept on precept; line on line, line on line; here a little, there a little*" (LITV).

It is interesting to observe that God is never mentioned anywhere in

---

[138] That it was the Holy Spirit infallibly speaking through those who penned the Scriptures, see, for example, Acts 1:16, Mark 12:36, and Matt. 1:22. Accordingly, after Jesus quoted a passage that contained teaching many He was speaking to might think shocking and objectionable, He reminded them, "*And the Scripture cannot be broken*" (John 10:35 NASB).

the book of Esther's ten chapters. But it would be wrong to draw a conclusion about God or God's Word based on that silence which is contradicted by passages in other books of the Bible. God is the author of every book in the Bible, including Esther. In the same way, even if there were no reference whatsoever to repentance in John,[139] that fact would not invalidate all of the teaching elsewhere in the Scriptures that we must repent and continue in repentance in order to inherit eternal life.

Here are some examples to demonstrate that general principle, which are taken from verses we have looked at about faith, repentance, and salvation.

As previously described, the first two transcripts of gospel messages preached to the unsaved after Jesus was raised from the dead explicitly mention only *repenting*, not *believing*, as necessary for salvation. We expect *repent* to appear in them because, as discussed in section 3.5, repentance is preached in the true gospel. Here are passages with those words from the two transcripts:

> Acts 2:37–38: Replying to the question, *"What shall we do?"* Peter answered, ***"Repent**, and each of you be baptized in the name of Jesus Christ for the forgiveness of your sins; and you will receive the gift of the Holy Spirit"* (NASB)

> Acts 3:19: *"Therefore **repent** and return [epistrepho: **turn**], so that your sins may be wiped away"* (NASB)

Conversely, we have Paul and Silas' famous answer in Acts 16:31 to the Philippian jailer's question, *"What must I do to be saved?"* (v. 30) that mentions only *believe* and not *repent*. (However, be aware that we do *not* have a transcript of their subsequent preaching the word of the Lord to him prior to it being said in v. 34 that he believed.) They answered:

---

[139] Hodges wrote on p. 130 of *Absolutely Free!* "the **doctrine** of repentance … is totally absent from John's Gospel," and it "omit[s] the **message** of repentance." (Emphasis added.)

> Acts 16:31–32: "*'Believe [inflected as a second person singular imperative] in the Lord Jesus, and you will be saved, you and your household.' And they spoke the word of the Lord to him*" (NASB)

In order to properly understand these passages, we need to interpret them in the context of each other and the rest of the Scriptures. Doing so keeps us from wrongly thinking that Acts 2:38 means that baptism by men in water is required to receive the gift of the Holy Spirit. Similarly, we do not wrongly think from Acts 16:31 that if one believes, members of one's household will be saved without believing.

All of the details, caveats, and nuances about a subject are not repeated in every verse in the Bible in which the subject is mentioned. We must interpret the words in a passage in a way that does not contradict what is plainly taught in other passages.

Accordingly, we should not interpret the first two of the three passages quoted above to teach that one must only repent, and need not believe in Jesus, in order to receive the Holy Spirit. Neither should we interpret the third passage to teach that one does not need to repent to be saved. Either interpretation would contradict the other passage(s), as well as numerous others in the Bible. In this specific case, such an interpretation of Acts 16:31 would even go to the extreme of having Paul contradict what we have seen *he himself* said about repentance and preached in this *same book* of Acts (for instance, in Acts 17:30–31, 20:21, and 26:16–20). But we can interpret these verses in a simple way in which there are no contradictions.

In section 3.2, "True Faith and Repentance Come Together," we saw that true faith will result in true repentance—one who truly believes in the Lord Jesus will repent and *will* be saved. Therefore, the statement in Acts 16:31 does not contradict the need to repent to be saved that is expressed in the first two passages.

We also saw in section 3.2 that *only* true faith results in and supports true repentance. Therefore, the first two verses do not indicate a way that someone may be saved without faith—as if one only needs to repent and may do so without believing! Rather, what those verses tell us must be done may *only* be done by those who truly believe. We can consider that the two commands to *"repent"* in them are implicitly prefaced with "if you now believe:" as if Peter answered, "If you now believe, repent, and each of you...," and as if he said, "Therefore, if you now believe, repent and turn, so that...."

The first two verses and the last verse are compatible, as they must be, though neither is complete and adequate by itself. Both faith and repentance are necessary to be saved (though there is no one who will truly have one without the other). Without setting aside that understanding, we can observe more about the Acts 16:31 answer and the Philippian jailer's salvation.

The account in Acts 16 shows us that the Philippian jailer was truly interested in pursuing their answer about how to be saved, for we see from the next verse that he took them to his house to hear about this Jesus. And there, *"they spoke the word of the Lord to him together with all who were in his house"* (v. 32 NASB).

His response to their initial answer that he should believe in someone he had never heard of, would not have been, "OK, I believe! Am I saved now?" But it could have been something like, "Who is the Lord Jesus, that I may believe in Him?" The only thing they had told the Philippian jailer about Jesus in their five word answer to his question was this attribute in His name—that He is called *"the Lord."*[140] For someone who has not heard of Jesus before, how notable that two-word attribute must be. Yet how fitting it is, and what else would one expect, since He is said to be the One who can save the jailer?

When they more fully *"spoke the word of the Lord to him,"* they told him about the Lord Jesus. They told the jailer about the One who[141]

---

[140] The Greek manuscripts used by the NKJV translators include a sixth word in their answer that contains another attribute: Christ.
[141] Whether or not they said any or all of these specific words, they told him *about* the One who **said** and **did** and **is** these things.

"died for our sins" (1 Cor. 15:3). They described the *"Christ"* who said, *"Unless you repent you will all likewise perish"* (Luke 13:5). They told him about the One who said, *"My sheep hear My voice ... and they follow Me"* (John 10:27 NASB), *"You are My friends if you do whatever I command you [a group that includes only those who have resolved and are trying to do whatever He commands, and none who are unrepentant]"* (John 15:14), and *"He who loves his life will lose it, and he who hates his life in this world will keep it for eternal life"* (John 12:25). Whoever believes in this One will be saved. And afterward, even that Philippian jailer *"believed in God"* (v. 34), together with his whole household.

In Paul's recorded preaching to the Athenians in the next chapter, Acts 17, he did not explicitly mention a need to believe, but rather only the command to repent *because* a day of God's judgment is coming: *"God ... now commands all men everywhere to repent, because He has appointed a day on which He will judge the world in righteousness by the Man whom He has ordained"* (vv. 30–31). Yet later, verse 34 says that some of the men who heard him believed, without explicitly mentioning whether they repented. There is no conflict between these verses within the Acts 17 passage.

As we have seen, it is not true that there is no "reference to repentance whatsoever" in John's Gospel. The three verses of Jesus' recorded words from John that were just quoted two paragraphs above—John 10:27, 15:14, and 12:25—are references to repentance. And Jesus' description in John 12:40 of what we must do to be saved refers to repentance using the word *turn*: *"They should **understand with their hearts** [receive it as true, believe] and **turn** [repent], so that I should heal them."*

Regardless, the Jesus described in John's Gospel is the same One who said all the things He is recorded to have said in Matthew, Mark, and Luke's Gospels.

"The fourth gospel says nothing at all about repentance, much less does it connect repentance in any way with eternal life."
As described, these statements are simply false. Further, the quoted John 12:25 comes alongside Luke 9:23–24 to make explicit what is

implied in the Luke passage—it is eternal life that is lost or saved based on whether someone continues in repentance.

"Only a resolute blindness can resist the obvious conclusion:"
There is no reasoning to address in this statement. Hodges simply states his judgment of *everyone*[142] who disagrees with him and *resists* his next-to-be-stated "conclusion:" They do so because they are determined to be blind, and there is nothing that can shake them from it—it is "a resolute blindness."

"*John did not regard repentance as a condition for eternal life.*"
This conclusion was based solely on reasoning from what was claimed to be *unmentioned* in *one* book of the Bible. The *reasoning* behind this conclusion was based on what was (supposedly) **not** written in John, and was also independent of **anything** that may have been written about repentance in the rest of the Bible. Said another way, the presented reasoning behind this conclusion is absolutely free of any basis in what **has been written** in the Bible.

The conclusion wrongly implies that what is written in John's Gospel is an expression of John's opinions ("John did not regard..."), and that his opinions may differ from opinions about this expressed by other writers of the New Testament (and his opinions carry more weight than theirs).[143] It is written as if the Jesus described and quoted in John's Gospel could be different from the One described and quoted in Luke's Gospel.

---

[142] Since he writes, "**Only** a resolute blindness can resist...[emphasis added]," meaning this must always be the case for anyone who resists.

[143] This is not the only place Hodges has worded things as if the Scriptures are not truly the words of God. For instance, just fourteen pages later, on p. 145 of *Absolutely Free!* he wrote to describe his understanding of a context behind the things that Luke penned in the book of Acts: "Paul, of course, was Luke's hero. ... And as Paul's sometimes traveling companion, Luke understood Pauline theology as well as anyone ever has. ... Luke knew that in Pauline theology...." Beware of this kind of teaching. **Nowhere** do the Scriptures talk about themselves or give precepts for how to interpret and understand them that are anything like this! The Bible is filled with God's truth, and the theology and "*the gospel of God*" (Rom. 1:1; 15:16; 1 Pet. 4:17; 2 Cor. 11:7) that are preached in it are **His**.

However, the Scriptures are the words of God, and John believed them all. John was only penning words given to him by the Holy Spirit that, when properly understood, are fully consistent with all that is written in the Scriptures. Also, he did so without necessarily fully understanding what he was writing himself.[144]

"If he had, he would have said so. After all, that's what his book is all about: obtaining eternal life (John 20:30-31)."
In addressing these statements, we will again ignore that we have seen John's Gospel shows repentance **is** a condition for obtaining eternal life.

Not only John's Gospel, but at least the majority of books in the Bible (including, perhaps, all books in the New Testament), are about "obtaining eternal life." And a number of them clearly show that repentance is a condition for obtaining eternal life.

A scriptural rule for establishing a matter is that there should be at least two or three witnesses,[145] and, of course, they should not be contradicted by other witnesses.[146] Accordingly, we should not base a doctrine on one verse of the Bible. Rather, we should have two or three verses, and our interpretation of them should not appear to be contradicted by two or three others. Correspondingly, God tells us in Proverbs 22:20–21, "*Have I not written to thee **three times** with counsels and knowledge? To cause thee to know **the certainty of sayings of truth**"* (YLT).

However, in this specific argument, **no witnesses** are offered which testify that repentance is not a condition for obtaining eternal life. The case is being made based on the (falsely claimed) **silence** of a particular witness. "**If** he had, he **would have said so.**" Surely, in the internal court in which we try and examine our personal beliefs, we should never reject the testimony of so many witnesses about a matter based on the *absence* of a particular witness' testimony or

---

[144] See, for example, 1 Pet. 1:10–12, Dan. 12:8–9, and 1 Cor. 8:2.
[145] See, for example, Deut. 19:15, Matt. 18:16, and 2 Cor. 13:1.
[146] Otherwise, two things could be "established" which contradict one another.

silence about the matter!

Appendix B

Reconciling Beliefs With Conflicting Scripture

*These were ... examining the Scriptures daily
to see whether these things were so.*
—Acts 17:11 NASB

Those who are following the Jesus who is described in the Bible seek to conform their understanding of all things to what they believe the Scriptures teach. Jesus taught that we should believe all things that are written in the Bible when He rebuked some of His disciples in Luke 24:25, saying, *"O foolish ones, and slow of heart to believe in all that the prophets have spoken!"* And He said in Luke 8:21, *"My brothers are these: the ones hearing the Word of God, and doing it"* (LITV).

However, it could be that someone finds an interpretation of one set of passages reasonable, but then is unable to reconcile the apparent teaching in those passages with the apparent teaching in other passages. In that situation, a person needs to answer the question, "How can I understand what *these* passages say in a compatible way with what these *other* passages say?"

Christians in that situation need to be careful they do not become *comfortable* with such contradictions in what they believe. Regrettably, some people appear to be settled in holding to a tenet that *in their own minds* is incompatible with some passages in the Bible. They may generally avoid or skip over those passages. But they may even become able to read them without noticing the conflict. And if the incompatibility between their tenet and those passages is raised, they may cavalierly acknowledge, "Yes, those are our 'problem passages!'"

Jesus' sheep hear His voice (John 10:3–5), and they seek to understand it and follow Him—entreating God for His help to do so. Of course, they should be more earnest to do so when the beliefs involved are more important.

When Christians notice passages that appear at odds with a tenet they hold, they may sometimes find that they are not able to point to passages which support their tenet. They may not even be able to articulate the tenet well. They may recollect that at some time in the past they heard or read things that seemed to thoroughly establish it, perhaps from a well-known Christian teacher.

It does not matter how Christians in any of these situations came to hold their tenet, or the basis for it. The only thing that ultimately matters is coming to a present understanding of what the Bible teaches about it. In the end, they should be able to articulate their understanding, point to passages in the Bible which teach it (for instance, those passages which particularly convinced them of their understanding), and explain how their confirmed or refined or new understanding is compatible with their understanding of other passages in the Scriptures.

But before we can honestly and fruitfully re-examine our beliefs in the light of the Scriptures, we need to be willing to hear what the Scriptures say, regardless of the earthly consequences to ourselves. If the personal cost of changing your beliefs could be significant, it is important to first settle in your heart that you are willing to change those beliefs if needed. As Luke 8:21 tells us, such a willingness is characteristic of all Jesus' brothers.

The following are the most important means of seeking a better understanding of anything in the Bible: 1) praying that God would give you an understanding, 2) having good reasons for wanting that understanding, and 3) seeking it diligently. Section 14.1 described those means in some detail. When praying to God for His help in something, it can be helpful to express that you are willing to accept a dreaded cost if it is necessary (as our Lord showed us in His prayers at Gethsemane).

When seeking a better understanding of something, we should be on the lookout for passages about it in our personal, daily reading of the Scriptures, and we should pay particular attention to them when encountered. Discussions with others may help us see what the Bible says about the issue, and where. Those discussions may be helpful whether those others have the same or different notions from our own.

The Bible records for our edification not only things which Jesus said, but also what His enemies asserted. It can help in discerning the Bible's teaching to see what the proponents of conflicting beliefs are saying, and how they reason.

A passage in John 7:45–52 gives an account of a dispute about whether Jesus was a deceiver or the Messiah. In it, we are presented with opinions and arguments from both sides.

Those who claimed Jesus was a deceiver (the chief priests and Pharisees) used scorn and derision to answer (that is, intimidate) those who were opposing: "*Have you not also been deceived?*" (v. 47 LITV) and, "*Are you also from Galilee?*" (v. 52 LITV) They pointed to the kind of people who held their belief to support their assertion: "*Not any from the rulers or from the Pharisees believed into Him have they?*" (v. 48 LITV) And they made an issue of where Jesus had come from: "*Search and see that a prophet has not been raised out of Galilee*" (v. 52 LITV). They did not describe anything Jesus had said or done that was contrary to the Scriptures, or that would show He could not be the Messiah according to the Scriptures.

By contrast, those who thought He might be the Messiah (the temple officers and Nicodemus) pointed to what Jesus was saying and doing, and tried (in vain) to get those who were opposing to consider those things: "*No man ever spoke like this Man!*" (v. 46) and, "*Does our law judge a man before it hears him and knows what he is doing?*" (v. 51)

The true help others can give us is in raising verses, and possibly offering interpretations or explanations of those verses, that enable us to better see what the Bible teaches about an issue. We should learn from the prophet Balaam's reproof by a donkey in Numbers 22:21–33. Even if a donkey points out some truth to us, we would do well to receive it.

Scripture Index

Romans

www.ingramcontent.com/pod-product-compliance
Lightning Source LLC
Chambersburg PA
CBHW071959040426
42447CB00009B/1403